THE BOOK OF QUESTIONS

EDMOND JABÈS

The Book
of Questions

Translated from the French by

ROSMARIE WALDROP

WESLEYAN UNIVERSITY PRESS

Middletown, Connecticut

Le Livre des Questions, the first volume of a trilogy of the same title, was originally published by Éditions Gallimard of Paris in 1963, and this English edition is published by arrangement with the French publisher. © 1963, Éditions Gallimard.

Acknowledgement is gratefully made to the editors of *Curtains, European Judaism, Modern Poetry in Translation, Sub/Stance,* and *Tree,* British and
American journals in which parts of this translation first appeared, and to the
Bonewhistle Press, the publisher of an anthology in which another part was
first published.
    I thank the author and, especially, Arlette Jabès for their invaluable help
and their suggestions. - R. W.

Library of Congress Cataloging in Publication Data

Jabès, Edmond, 1912–
    The book of questions.

    Translation of Le livre des questions.
    I. Title.
PQ2619.A112L513   848'.9'1407   75-34058
ISBN 0-8195-4091-9 (v. 1)
ISBN 0-8195-6043-x (v.1) pbk.

Manufactured in the United States of America
First English edition

CONTENTS

THE BOOK OF QUESTIONS

DEDICATION

TO THE REMOTE SOURCES OF LIFE AND DEATH REVEALED.

TO THE DUST OF THE WELL.

TO THE RABBI-POETS IN WHOSE MOUTHS I PUT MY WORDS AND WHOSE
NAMES HAVE, OVER THE CENTURIES, BECOME MINE.

TO SARAH AND YUKEL.

TO THOSE, FINALLY, WHOSE ROADS OF INK AND BLOOD GO THROUGH
WORDS AND MEN.

AND, MOST OF ALL, TO YOU. TO US. TO YOU.

You are the one who writes and the one who is written.

At the Threshold of the Book

> *Mark the first page of the book with a red marker. For, in the beginning, the wound is invisible.*
>
> —Reb Alcé

1

"I gave you my name, Sarah. And it is a dead end road."
—Yukel's Journal

"I scream. I scream, Yukel. We are the innocence of the scream."
—Sarah's Journal

2

"What is going on behind this door?"

"A book is shedding its leaves."

"What is the story of the book?"

"Becoming aware of a scream."

"I saw rabbis go in."

"They are privileged readers. They come in small groups to give us their comments."

"Have they read the book?"

"They are reading it."

"Did they happen by for the fun of it?"

"They foresaw the book. They are prepared to encounter it."

"Do they know the characters?"

"They know our martyrs."

"Where is the book set?"

"In the book."

"Who are you?"

"I am the keeper of the house."

"Where do you come from?"

"I have wandered."

"Is Yukel your friend?"

"I am like Yukel."

"What is your lot?"

"To open the book."

"Are you in the book?"

"My place is at the threshold."

"What have you tried to learn?"

"I sometimes stop on the road to the sources and question the signs, the world of my ancestors."

"You examine recaptured words."

"The nights and mornings of the syllables which are mine, yes."

"Your mind is wandering."

"I have been wandering for two thousand years."

"I have trouble following you."

"I, too, have often tried to give up."

"Do we have a tale here?"

"My story has been told so many times."

"What is your story?"

"Ours, insofar as it is absent."

"I do not understand."

"Speaking tortures me."

"Where are you?"

"In what I say."

"What is your truth?"

"What lacerates me."

"And your salvation?"

"Forgetting what I said."

"May I come in? It is getting dark."

"In each word there burns a wick."

"May I come in? It is getting dark around my soul."

"It is dark around me, too."

"What can you do for me?"

"Your share of luck is in yourself."

"Writing for the sake of writing does nothing but show contempt."

"Man is a written bond and place."

"I hate what is said in places I have left behind."

"You trade in the future, which is immediately translated. What you have left is you without you."

"You oppose me to myself. How could I ever win this fight?"

"Defeat is the price agreed on."

"You are a Jew, and you talk like one."

"The four letters JUIF which designate my origin are your four fingers. You can use your thumb to crush me."

"You are a Jew, and you talk like one. But I am cold. It is dark. Let me come into the house."

"There is a lamp on my table. And the house is in the book."

"So I will live in the house after all."

"You will follow the book, whose every page is an abyss where the wing shines with the name."

"There are no steps in the sea nor degrees in pain."
—Reb Youré

"Universe pulled from sleep together with words—at every age of the book, a dawn separates out the leveled forms."
—Reb Tal

"To see is to go through mirrors.
At the end: The night of the last star."
—Reb Elar

"There is the Book of God, through which God questions himself. And there is the book of man. It is on the scale of God's."
—Reb Rida

"A minute is enough to know a century."
—Reb Kelat

"My book has seven days and seven nights times the number of years it took the universe to let it go."
—Reb Aloum

"The book is as old as water and fire."
—Reb Rafan

4

("He is a Jew," said Reb Tolba. "He is leaning against a wall, watching the clouds go by."

"The Jew has no use for clouds," replied Reb Jalé. "He is counting the steps between him and his life.")

And You Shall Be in the Book

> *When, as a child, I wrote my name for the
> first time, I knew I was beginning a book.*
> — Reb Stein

("What is light?" one of his disciples asked Reb Abbani.

"In the book," replied Reb Abbani, "there are unsuspected large blank spaces. Words go there in couples, with one single exception: the name of the Lord. Light is in these lovers' strength of desire.

"Consider the marvelous feat of the storyteller, to bring them from so far away to give our eyes a chance."

And Reb Hati: "The pages of the book are doors. Words go through them, driven by their impatience to regroup, to reach the end of the work, to be again transparent.

"Ink fixes the memory of words to the paper.

"Light is in their absence, which you read.")

Do I know, at this hour when men lift their eyes up to the sky, when knowledge claims a richer, more beautiful part of the imagination (all the secrets of the universe are buds of fire soon to open), do I know, in my exile, what has driven me back through tears and time, back to the wells of the desert where my ancestors had ventured? There is nothing at the threshold of the open page, it seems, but this wound of a race born of the book, whose order and disorder are roads of suffering. Nothing but this pain, whose past and whose permanence is also that of writing.

The word is bound to the word, never to man, and the Jew to his Jewish world. The word carries the weight of each of its letters, as the Israelite has, from the first dawn, carried that of his image.

Water marks the boundaries of oases. Between one tree and another, there is all the thirst of the earth.

"I am the word. And you claim to know me by my face," said Reb Josué, one day, to a rabbi come to meet him, indignant that the inspired man should be known by his features.

A town at night is a shopwindow emptied of things.

A few graffiti on a wall were enough for the dormant memories in my hand to take over my pen, for my fingers to determine what I see.

The story of Sarah and Yukel is the account, through various dialogues and meditations attributed to imaginary rabbis, of a love destroyed by men and by words. It has the dimensions of the book and the bitter stubbornness of a wandering question.

> ("The soul is a moment of light, which the first word can touch off. Then we are like the universe with thousands of heavenly bodies on our skin. You know them apart by the intensity of their radiance, as you tell a star by the clarity of its avowal."
>
> —Reb Aber

> "Distance is light, as long as you keep in mind that there are no limits.
> "We are distance."
>
> —Reb Mirshak)

They are gathered around him like rabbis around the lamp after sundown.

"Ah," says Reb Amon, "when I come back to my lamp I am all ears. Its knowledge has shaped mine."

And Yukel says: "He followed me through the streets of Paris. And he knew my story by heart.

"He followed me into my past of shadow and light, into my confused thinking, into my lack of a future.

"He sometimes usurped my name.

"But I am not this man.

"Because this man writes,
and the writer is nobody."

(The alley (a dead end) could have gone all across town, if they had let it. A wall blocked its way. And behind the wall, tall buildings, which time had dressed in mourning. The alley struggled in a rectangle of stone like the book in its bounds of ink and paper, under its worn cover.

For the writer, discovering the work he will write is both like a miracle and a wound, like the miracle of the wound.

It seemed to me I had for centuries shuttled between life and death (the life and death of my race) to end up at this place to be born.

I let words take their place in my book. I fol-

lowed them with my finger. They came in twos and, sometimes, in fives or tens. I respected the moving order they entered me with. I knew I had been carrying this book within me for a long time.

Far from the harbor, the boat grew larger. As I faced the open sea, my book became the single place where all roads cross and urge us on. But a scream went through me. And on this scream I built my suffering to sail from ocean to ocean.)

3

"You dream of having a place in the book and, right away, you become a word shared by eyes and lips."

— Reb Seni

"Signs and wrinkles are questions and answers of the same ink."

— *Je bâtis ma demeure*

"You chose," said Reb Eloda. "Now you are at the mercy of your choice.

"But did you choose to be Jewish?"

And Reb Ildé: "What is the difference between choosing and being chosen, since we cannot help submitting to choice?"

"You are silent: I was. You speak: I am."

— Reb Moline

4

(If the sea had no waves to uproot it and give it back to the sea, if the sea had too many waves (but not enough) to overrun the horizon, enough (but just barely) to disturb the earth, if the sea had no ears to hear the sea, no eyes to be forever the look of the sea, if the sea had neither salt nor foam, it would be a grey sea of death in the sun cut off from its roots. It would be a dying sea amid branches cut off from the sun. It would be a mined sea whose explosions would threaten the world in its elephant memory. But the fruit. What would become of the fruit? But man. What would become of man?)

5

("If we have been created to endure the same suffering, to be doomed to the same prearranged death: why give us lips, why eyes and voices, why souls and languages all different?"
— Reb Midrash)

To be in the book. To figure in the book of questions, to be part of it. To be responsible for a word or a sentence, a stanza or chapter.

To be able to say: "I am in the book. The book is my world, my country, my roof, and my riddle. The book is my breath and my rest."

I get up with the page that is turned. I lie down with the page put down. To be able to reply: "I belong to the race of words, which homes are built with" — when I know full well that this answer is still another question, that this home is constantly threatened.

I will evoke the book and provoke the questions.

If God is, it is because He is in the book. If sages, saints, and prophets exist, if scholars and poets, men and insects exist, it is because their names are found in the book. The world exists because the book does. For existing means growing with your name.

The book is the work of the book. It is the sun, which gives birth to the sea. It is the sea, which reveals the earth. It is the earth, which shapes man. Otherwise, sun, sea, earth, and man would be focused light without object, water moving without going or coming, wealth of sand without presence, a waiting of flesh and spirit without touch, having nothing that corresponds to it, having neither doubles nor opposites.

Eternity ticks off the instant with the word.

The book multiplies the book.

Yukel, you have never felt at ease in your skin. You have never been *here*, but always *elsewhere*, ahead of yourself or behind like winter in the eyes of autumn or summer in the eyes of spring, in the past or in the future like those syllables whose passage from night to day is so much like lightning that it merges with the movement of the pen.

The present is, for you, this passage too rapid to be seized. What is left of the passage of the pen is the word, with its branches and leaves green or already dead. The word hurled into the future in order to translate it.

You read the future. You give us the future to read. Yet yesterday, you were not. And tomorrow, you will no longer be.

And yet you have tried to incrust yourself in the present, to be that unique moment when the pen holds the word which will survive.

You have tried.

You cannot say what your steps want, where they lead you. One never knows very well where the adventure begins and where it ends. And yet it begins in a certain place and ends some place farther off, at a precise point.

At a certain hour. On a certain day.

Yukel, you have gone through dreams and through time. For those who see you (but they do not see you — I see you) you are a shape moving in the fog.

Who were you, Yukel?

Who are you, Yukel?

Who will you be?

"You" means, sometimes, "I."

I say "I," and I am not "I." "I" means you, and you are going to die. You are drained.

From now on, I will be alone.

> *(Have you ever seen blind legs, arms, a blind neck?*
>
> *Have you ever seen blind lips? Like those of the man taking a walk this evening, this last evening*
>
> *at the end of his life.*
>
> *Yukel, have I been the sight you lack, the sight of your foot on the tile, of your arms in the embrace, of your neck in thirst? The sight of your lips kissing and speaking?*
>
> *"I" means you. You are going to die. And I will be alone.)*

You are walking toward death. It has spared you till now, so that you should go towards it of your own accord. You are walking on all the deaths which belong to you and your race, on the obscure sense and the lack of sense of all these deaths.

And it is I who force you to walk. I sow your steps.

And I think, I speak for you. I choose and cadence.

For I am writing

and you are the wound.

Have I betrayed you, Yukel?

I have certainly betrayed you.

Between earth and sky, I have kept nothing but the childish opening of your pain. You are one of the grains of the collective scream which the sun paints golden.

I have given your name and Sarah's to this stubborn scream,

to this scream wedded to its breath and older than any of us,

to this everlasting scream

older than the seed.

Forgive me, Yukel. I have substituted my inspired sentences for yours. You are the toneless utterance among anecdotal lies. An utterance like a star engulfed among stars. In the evening, only my stars will be seen, only their warm and wonderful sparkle. But just for the time of your brief vanishing. Returning, you will take your place again. Silent.

How could you have expressed yourself, when you open your mouth only to prolong the scream? How could you have the desire and the patience to explain your steps,

when you are without desire or patience?

Who are you, Sarah, in Yukel's springtime?

> (*Where the blood of the earth is rounder than the earth, where dawn, to clothe her, weaves the flax,*
> *where she is,*
> *where water endlessly drips from her toes: can we know what happens to a woman pulled out of the water,*
> *separated from the simple life of her hands, from the joys of the waves?*
> *They have cut her to pieces.*
> *She is prey to their ropes.*)

Who are you, Yukel, in Sarah's springtime?

> (*Do you ask your shadow what became of it during the night?*
> *Or ask the night about your shadow?*)

You were the night. And you walk towards the night. You miss it because you know how gentle it is, how cooling its palm on your eyes. Day was all pain for you, night, recreation. And nevertheless you dream of light, of fields, of horizons of light.

"Is it true," the innocent Maimoun asked Reb Nati, one day, "is it true I was born with the first man?"

"You were born with the first divine wish," replied Reb Nati. "And this wish was that you should be a man."

"Is it true," the innocent Maimoun asked again, "that loving God means loving Him in men?"

"Loving God," answered Reb Nati, "means making your own His love of men.

"God is an unobtrusive wick, which will be light through you. It waits under glass for the gesture of fire which makes it your lamp."

"In this case, I have lost my God," groaned the innocent Maimoun. "I do not love the men who killed my father. And since then, I have lived in the dark."

Who are you, Sarah, in Yukel's winter?

> *(Doe tracked down in the maze of asphalt and lead, which I am walking through tonight. Doe caught alive to be burned (you escaped the fire of men, but not your own), led off by the hunters of your country to be given up to the receivers of your stolen freedom, the butchers of your light step, your open arms.*
>
> *Sarah, all white,*
> *like the wall the graffiti nail you to,*
> *like the sea, which turns into words of love wherever you go,*
> *Sarah of wandering.)*

Who are you, Yukel, in Sarah's winter?

You are my companion with your invisible crown of thorns. You are no hero and not quite a citizen. Kept in the background by your kind. I accompanied you through your school books, where your lot was traced in pencil, through your later note books, illegible with erasures.

One after the other, I retrieved all the sentences I could not read. (But did you write them? Did you say them? Did you only think them?)

I let ink run into the body of every letter I guessed, so that it should live and die of its own sap,

which is yours, Yukel, in the book,

in what the book approaches and conceals.

"Whosoever does not believe in the book," said Reb Gandour, "has lost faith in man and in the kingdom of man."

Is there, brother, a word dreamier and more alert, more miserable and more fraternal than the one you incarnate?

6

"Our ties to beings and things are so fragile they often break without us noticing."

"A breath, a glance, a sign, and sometimes just confiding a shadow: such is, roughly, the original nature of our ties."

"If our ties are eternal, it is because they are divine."

"You try to be free through writing. How wrong. Every word unveils another tie."

— Reb Léca

"I name you. You were."

— Reb Vita

You have a name you did not ask for. All your life, this name will prey on you.
But at which moment do you become aware of it?

> *(If your name has only one letter, you are at the threshold of your name.*
> *If your name has two letters, two doors open your name.*
> *If your name has three letters, three masts carry off your name.*

*If your name has four letters, four horizons
drown your name.*

*If your name has five letters, five books blow
the leaves off your name.*

*If your name has six letters, six sages interpret
your name.*

*If your name has seven letters, seven branches
burn your name.)*

You have the void for face.

"Child, the letters of your name are so far apart that you are
a bonfire in the starry night.

"In time, you will feel the dimensions of your name, the anguish of the nothing you answer to."

— Reb Amiel

You have the void for voyage.

"Once you have taken possession of your name, the alphabet is yours. But soon you will be the slave of your riches."

— Reb Teris

"You take on yourself the sin of the book."

— Reb Levi

7

THE COMMENTARIES OF THE RABBIS AB, TEN, ZAM, ELAR, DABER, ELATI, AND YUKEL'S SECOND SPEECH

> *"Do not neglect the echo. You live by echoes."*
> —Reb Prato

The commentary of Reb Ab:

"A writer's life takes its sense through what he says, what he writes, what can be handed down from generation to generation.

"What is remembered is sometimes only one phrase, one line.

"There is the truth.

"But what truth?

"If a phrase or line survives the work, it is not the author who gave it this special chance (at the expense of the others): it is the reader.

"There is the lie.

"The writer steps aside for the work, and the work depends on the reader.

"So truth is, in time, the absurd and fertile quest of lies, which we pay with tears and blood."

("*You, who think I exist,*
how can I tell you what I know
with words which mean
more than one thing,
with words like me, which change
when looked at,
words with an alien voice?
How can I say
that I am not,
yet in every word
I see,
I hear,
I understand myself?
How say all this to you
whose new reality
is that of the light
by which
the world
knows the world
while losing you?
And yet you answer
to a borrowed
name?
How can I show what I create,
outside myself,
page after page,
when doubt
erases
every trace of my passage?
Who ever saw
the images I give?
Last of all, I claim my due.
But how prove my innocence
when the eagle rose from my hand
to conquer the sky
which hugs me?
I die of pride
at the end of my strength.
What I await is always farther.
How could I make you part

of my adventure,
when it is the avowal of
my loneliness
and of the road?")

The commentary of Reb Ten:

"My road had its hours of greatness,
its blows, its pain.
My road has its crest and its groundswell,
its sand and its sky.
My road. Yours."

("I do not know
if you were taught
that the earth is round
like thirst.
And that,
when lovers' shadows move
at the approach of dawn,
the poet's tongue,
the tongue of wells and centuries,
is dry,
is rough and dry.
It has done so much service
and disservice,
has been so long exposed to the air,
to the noise,
to its own words,
that it has hardened,
glazed,
and crumbled.
After the road,
and before the road,
there are stones
and ashes on scattered stones.
The book
rises out of the fire

of the prophetic rose,
from the scream of the sacrificed petals.
Smoke.
Smoke
for all who see only fire,
who smell only
dawn
and death.
But the order of summits,
the order or ruins,
is wedding gladness.")

The commentary of Reb Zam:

"You enter the night,
as a thread enters the needle,
through an opening
propitious or bloody,
through the most luminous breach.
Being both thread and needle,
you enter the night
as you enter yourself."

The commentary of Reb Elar:

"From one word to another,
possible void,
far,
irresistible.
Dream the instalment,
the small,
the first one down.

You can retrace a road in your mind
or your veins.

You can dig a road in men's eyes.
The child is the master of roads.

Descend.
Melt and melt into
the fall,
oblivion,
which is falling of things
and beings.
With the weight
that has found its weight
for dying."

Yukel, how many pages to live, to die, are between you and yourself,
    between the book and leaving the book?

And Yukel speaks:

I look for you.
The world where I look for you is a world without trees.
Nothing but empty streets,
naked streets.
The world where I look for you is a world open to other
    worlds without name,
a world where you are not, where I look for you.
There are your steps,
steps which I follow and wait for.
I followed the slow road of your steps without shadow,
unaware who I was,
unaware where I went.
One day, you will be there.
Here, elsewhere, it will be
a day like all the days when you are there.

Perhaps tomorrow.
To find you, I followed yet other bitter roads
where salt broke salt.
To find you, I followed other hours, other banks.
Night gives its hand to him who follows the night.
At night, all the roads fall.
There had to be this night when I took your hand, when
    we were alone.
There had to be this night, as there had to be this
    road.
In the world where I look for you, you are both grass
    and ore.
You are the scream lost where I lose my way.
You are also, where nothing wakes, oblivion with
    ashes of mirror.

The commentary of Reb Daber:

"The road which leads me to you is safe even when it runs into oceans."

"How can I know if I write verse or prose," Reb Elati re-marked. "I am rhythm."

And elsewhere: "Without rhythm, you would not see the sun every morning.

"You could not.

"Rhythm is internal. It is the rhythm of fate.

"No matter how you tried, you could neither go faster nor more slowly.

"You could not but move in harmony with your blood, with your mind, with your heart.

"In harmony.

"You could not be fast or slow.

"You could not.

"Is it conceivable for the moon to come after the moon?

"I went to God, because God was my fate.

"I went to the word of God, because the word of God was my fate.

"I went to the word

"to make it my gesture.

"I went.

"And I am going."

The Book of the Absent

First Part

All letters give form to absence.
Hence, God is the child of His Name.
— Reb Tal

1

*A child can cause more harm than an adult, an
adult more than a child: vicious circle, this original circle.
One with chalk, the other with the sword.*

But what stops him? What makes him suddenly think? An
unimportant incident which will not change the course of his
life, will not change anything.

A pebble in the stream.

Did he walk through unfamiliar districts? Some man, in
passing, bumped against his shoulder in a crowded street. Was
it yesterday? Today? Where was it? It must have been far from
his room. He walked by couples embracing like young trees
that take root in the sky and are laden with stars. He passed a
woman who asked him . . . He did not answer her. He had not
heard what she said. He had only heard sounds. He had not
even seen her. Had he really passed her? He heard noises . . .
noises. He walked through red lights, through green lights.
He followed, lost, came back to, followed the street lamps. He
caught bits of conversation, forgot them, remembered them
again together with an idea, a thought, a project. He walked.
He is walking. He does not want to go back home. He does not
have the courage. He follows the current. To find his room he
would have to make an effort, remember, take a direction, find
out the time and where he was. He does not have the energy.

He drifts. The wind blows for him, in him, behind him. So many dead leaves in his heart and at his feet. So many sails hoisted and torn. He stumbles. It is not only tiredness that makes him stumble or, rather, yes. But a millennial tiredness heavier than a burden. A weariness that saps his strength. There are so many roads he has taken. And they are all one and the same road.

How to explain, how? He has never been able to. The word and he are strangers. He is not talkative. He has so much to say that he has never formulated: simple things, like how do you do, which would please some people, things which are not thought of any more, which are perhaps forgotten. Things which would put others to shame.

Now it is too late.

He thinks of those African water mills turned by a buffalo with blinders over her eyes. He thinks of this humiliated animal that waters the ground, turning forever around herself, awkward, docile, and gives water to man who humiliates her.

He feels close to her.

He walks. He still has that pain in his neck.

"There are winners," said the imprisoned rabbi, the imprisoned saint. "Winners with their arrogance, their eloquence. And there are losers without words and without signs.

"The race of the silent is tenacious."

The rabbi's ashes are over there, in arable soil, and the rabbi's words in the town.

What could be more real than these streets he walks (if he walks he is alive), than this capital he passes through, eyes closed, or eyes wide open? What could be more real than this irreality, this unreal reality, whose master he is and whose puppet,

as the captain is master on board?

He is obsessed by a face with closely cropped blond hair which the barber keeps at a respectful distance from the neck (a fighter's neck) and will not let cover the temples. A face with nearsighted eyes looking out between rusty pins—the

kind of pins used to hold together batches of notes on graph
paper, elevated to the dignity of a police dossier.

"Pins are the surest ties. With time, they become part of the
page, grow into it. And they prick whoever tries to undo their
work."

The patience of the scream has no limits. It outlasts martyrdom.

The patience of the scream has no merit.

No institution, no government has a monopoly on the
scream.

No career, no crest, no wave either.

Here, which is elsewhere (elsewhere chained to our ankles), it is not one country that the scream accuses, nor one
continent, but the whole world. It is not one man, but all.

It is not one rosary the scream indicts, nor one chapel, but
hundreds of chapels and millions of rosaries. It is not one
hymn or one prayer. It is not one herb or one waxing moon.

> (*It is one country and one herb. It is one rosary
> and one continent. It is one prayer and one
> hymn. It is one waxing earth and moon.*)

The impatience of the scream is its merit.

"In the eyes of eternity," said Reb Moussa, "our patience is
unreasoned impatience."

> (*What is taught by the branches
> men in turn teach
> to the branches.
> What is sung by the sea
> men in turn sing
> to the sea.
> All this joy, this being at home:
> Is there nothing we have spared?*)

I will not avenge you, Sarah. What does your name mean to others? You had a name for my love and a name for the dawn. But you will be avenged.

You are the conscience and the truth nobody likes to hear. The truth which is judgment.

One day, people will know that beauty had your face, your clouds, and your grey sky.

Car beams light up the front of a building. (In which street? There are so many behind and before him that he cannot remember). He reads:

MORT AUX JUIFS

JEWS GO HOME

scrawled in white chalk, in caps.

In which street? In several streets. On several walls. He tried to decipher all the graffiti. He read and reread:

MORT AUX JUIFS

at each halt, at each corner, at the same corner, at each halt.

All he saw any more were those three words on the walls. (Perhaps they did not even exist — I mean, for the other passers-by). All he saw any more were those twelve letters, transparent, on the glass pane of his memory.

There have been sirens tracing an arch of anguish into the slithery air. There have been shells exploding around a man and in his flesh. There has been many an exodus on land and on sea, with solitary returns to pillaged rooms or to the heart of a soul long put to other uses.

There have been graveyards, with grass over them, vast fields. The flowers are in cahoots. They have fed on bones and on bone thoughts. Their perfume is perjured.

"My God," he murmurs. "The hands of the years show always the same hour."

pen would be unusable by now, choked with rust. His hand unreflected in any word, any letter. It would not have formed any image in ink. As for his eyes, they would have foundered on the page closed to them, uninvited at any moment of their passage. Only writing can keep the writer's eyes on the surface.

He follows the course of his eyes. He questions. He does not have the time to answer. So many questions turn away from his tongue, race along his arm towards his palm. So many desires push the pen, give his fingers the strength to push the pen.

Where is the path? It must each time be discovered anew. A blank sheet is full of paths. You know you must go from left to right. You know there will be much walking, much effort. And always from left to right. You also know beforehand (at least sometimes) that once the page is black with signs you will tear it up. You will walk the same way ten times, a hundred times: the pathway of your nose, of your neck, of your mouth, the pathway of your forehead, and of your soul. All these ways have their own ways. Else they would not be ways.

Having our paths (or our possible paths) mapped out for us, why do we usually take the one which leads us away from our goal, leads us elsewhere, where we are not? But perhaps we are there also? Only when guided by inspiration do we choose right, when we are receptive, in a state of grace. But that is rare, even very rare. And those who are (in the state of grace) do not know it. I mean, at the time. The more so, since being in the state of grace often means losing your way, your usual way, in order to follow another: more secret, more mysterious.

We all have our routes mapped out. And, on the unfolded map of knowledge, the longest are the shortest. He had experienced this recently. One afternoon, he had ventured into the desert which spreads in the East, beyond the frontiers of the Middle-Eastern country where his parents lived. He needed a landscape to fit his loneliness. He drove his car in various directions. He plunged in to the limits of safety. Around him, a warm night took off her bracelets and necklaces. – The most amazing one was pink. — He marveled that she seemed to appear and disappear, multiply and, suddenly, become so small he could hold her in his arms. He admired the night for being a woman and a whole female world, for being naked and dressed in stars.

Now and then, the wind softly brushed over the shadow and its bed, furtively, like a scout, and was gone again. Nothing indicated with what violence it would, by sunrise, attack that particle of the void where he had taken refuge. Nothing. For up to that very moment, the sand did not drop its indifference.

— But perhaps that is exactly why?

At noon, he found himself facing the infinite, the blank page. All tracks, footprints, paths were gone. Buried. He had pitched a tent on arriving: how come it had not blown off? From inside, he watched the complex improvisations of the wind. He heard how it suddenly laughed with the sand, danced with the sand, amused and irritated the sand, amused itself and got irritated with the number of grains. And finally, it became, in its desire, a mad sand god dragging monstrous winged creatures off to conquer the world.

He was probably only a few dozen miles from his point of departure. But he did not know. And how could one, here, speak of arrival or departure? Everywhere: oblivion, the unmade bed of absence, the wandering kingdom of dust.

Man's salvation is whatever has, as he has, a beginning and an end, whatever can start over. Salvation is the water that quenches our thirst only to be needed again. It is the bread which satisfies and maintains our hunger. It is what sprouts, develops, ripens for man and with him. Eternity, the infinite, are enemies of pulp and rind. When there is nothing left, there will still be sand. There will still be the desert to conjugate the nothing.

In the heart of what no longer is moved nor takes root, in the heart of the self-contained that defies reason and seasons (the keys of the desert surrender the five continents), in the heart of these arid stretches which repelled the sea as slowness overcame them (slowness is a formidable power: it has the passion of immobility with which it will, some day, fuse), in the heart of the irrevocable refusal to be (because living means acknowledging one's limits) man is like a prisoner in jail: he is finally conscious of his loss, the victory of his loss. What can you do against a wall? You tear it down. What can you do against bars? You file them. But a wall of sand? Bars which are our shadows on sand? When the goal is always yet farther away, there is no advance.

The infinite has the transparency of evil. Whatever goes beyond us despises us. Whatever escapes us destroys us. Wherever the birds fly low in order to see their shape, the sky has pushed off the dunes, and death set up reign, welcomed by the meek landmarks of death.

For all that, he was not in danger. He simply had to get back to the sea on foot. His car was no help, with its motor logged by the sandstorm and its wheels bogged down.

He made a plan. He would start out at sundown. But until then? The heat was scorching. He decided to lie down in his tent. His head hurt. He would rest every two hours. He would trust his instinct for the direction and shortcuts.

March winds act like falcons which, if there are enough of them, knock you down after pecking out your eyes. He imagined a blind world, completely at their mercy. Would he find the beach, his house?

His heart beat regularly, as if a source were hollowing out a path through his chest. He clung to his heart, as if to hold on to the source. He clung to any symbol, any naive image of life. Poor man, he had no idea he was turning away from himself.

To recover, after each blow, the original balance of life and death, to sacrifice to one as to the other, to one after the other, to be dead with death and living with life up to your last sigh (which is not death's triumph, but forsaking the body): this is health.

As an adolescent he had gone through the first, painful apprenticeship of death. He had seen it close by. He had stood at its bedside. Death speaks our language. In order to be understood it comes down to our level — or lifts us up to the level of catastrophe, and even lends us its own voice. Bending over his sister's bed, he had heard her going much beyond his juvenile revolt, revealing to him the far side of things, the territory of chance.

To answer the dying girl he had used, as she had, words prompted by death—the only ones which could unite them. When they fell silent, he understood that he had lost her.

Likewise with leaves and with sand. The dialogue cannot, must not be interrupted. Dialogue of the living with the leaves—dialogue of the dead with the sand.

He let go, by and by. Death had become his task. He entered into the system which is the condition of existence. He discovered its close and precise functioning. Like the body, the soul needs to be taken care of. And the soul is hungry for the bread of life and death.

He remembered the answer Reb Aaron gave to a strange rabbi come to question his teaching:

"He who lives within himself, beside his God, beside the life and death of God, lives in two adjoining rooms with a door between. He goes from one to the other in order to celebrate Him. He goes from presence in consciousness to presence in absence. He must fully be, before he can aspire to not being any more, that is to say: to being more, to being all. For absence is All."

He died for each second. He gathered a strength from beyond the grave. He was a fraction of the desert and an inflection of the wind. He stripped the untouched page of its leaves.

But the word is a triumphant sower. Dawn and dusk are written, as is race. When he got back to his neighborhood, to his house (a nomad had taken him on his camel to the nearest control post where he caught a military truck to town), so many words urged him. He was, however, bent on avoiding them. They were still too much in love with space for him to think of fixing them.

3

I believe in the writer's mission. He receives it from the word, which carries its suffering and its hope within it. He questions the words, which question him. He accompanies the words, which accompany him. The initiative is shared, as if spontaneous. Being useful to them (in using them) he gives a deep sense to his life and to theirs, from which his own has sprung.

That time is far, yet too near.
I, Serafi, the absent, am born to write books.

(I am absent because I am the teller. Only the tale is real.)

I have traveled around the world of absence.

I have spoken to my absent-minded fellow men in their language (which is their prey, and of which they are prey),

to my fellow men who have not always considered me their fellow man.

I have borne the weight of their prey.

I have erased, in my books, the borderline of life and death.

I have taken leave.

You had no idea, mother, that in conceiving me you bequeathed to the broad day pages of flesh and light for all the

sentences which are tattoos I would be called to defend, for all
the sentences which are banderoles and insects.

You cut to the quick of the scream.

(The well I draw from is on Jewish land.
My story is born in this well.

The well I draw from is on Jewish land.
My brothers sit on its edge.
They have drunk of the water of their land.
I bring you back this well.

My story is born in the well.
At first, it was pure cool water.
My brothers have lost their well.
My brothers have wept for their well.

I bring you back this well.)

"Yukel, which is this land you call Jewish, which every Jew
claims as his own without ever having lived there?"

"It is the land where I have dug my well."

"Yukel, which is this water of our land, so good against thirst
that no other water can compare?"

"It is the water fifty centuries have forgotten in the hollow
of our hands."

"Open your hands, brothers," wrote Reb Segré. "And bury
your faces in them. They will thrive like plants touching water."

"My thumb is a fierce guardian," said Reb Hakim. "My index quickest to recognize the evening star. My middle finger,
most distant, is the dream that undoes the shores. My ring fin-

ger wears our oaths and chains at its base. Sounds live in my
little finger and clothe it in diamonds.

"I like the index best. It is always ready to dry a tear."

Have my books added to the misunderstanding between me
and my brothers? They have turned hope into despair.

> (*The first phrases of a work are always full of
> hope. Doubt creeps in and blossoms on the way.
> At the end, there is double despair: that of the
> writer and that of the witness.*)

In the course of my wakings, I have traveled over the map of
both hemispheres without finding rest.

> (*As I am absent, only the map is real.*)

I have been around.
I have circled around myself without finding rest.

My brothers turned to me and said:
"You are not Jewish. You do not go to the synagogue."

I turned to my brothers and answered:
"I carry the synagogue within me."

My brothers turned to me and said:
"You are not Jewish. You do not pray."

I turned to my brothers and answered:
"Prayer is my backbone and my blood."

My brothers turned to me and said:

"The rabbis you quote are charlatans. Did they even exist? And you feed on their ungodly words."

I turned to my brothers and answered:

"The rabbis I quote are beacons of my memory. One can only remember oneself. And you know that the soul has words as petals."

The oldest of my brothers turned to me and said:

"Our Purim is no longer the feast of your carnival and your joy. Passover no longer the anniversary of your halt in the desert, your passage through the sea. Yom Kippur no longer your day of fasting.

"These dates marked in our calendar: what do they mean to you now?

"Rejected by your people, robbed of your heritage: who are you?

"For the others, you are a Jew, but hardly for us."

I turned to the oldest of my brothers and answered:

"I have the wound of the Jew. I was circumcised, as you were, on the eighth day after my birth. I am a Jew, as you are, in each of my wounds.

"But is one man not as good as another?"

The most thoughtful of my brothers turned to me and said:

"If you make no difference between a Jew and a non-Jew, are you, in fact, still a Jew?"

My brothers turned to me and continued:

"Brotherhood does not mean putting yourself in your neighbor's place. It means you take into account what he is, but you want him to be as he should be, as the holy texts require he be, even at the risk of hurting him.

"It is the goal that counts. The most imaginative are the most brotherly.

"The believer's intransigence is like a razor blade: it cuts."

And they added:

"Brotherhood means giving, giving, giving. And you can only give what you are."

I beat my breast with my fist and thought:

"I am nothing.

"My head is cut off.

"But is one man not as good as another?

"The beheaded as good as the believer?"

4

My books are made to be read first, then told.
That is why I call them tales.

(We are joined together by all the words, whose
desire we are."

— Reb Veil)

Do you remember the first stanza of the song Reb Ephraim
wrote in honor of his teachers?

> "A door—a book.
> Open. Closed.
> You pass. You read.
> You pass. It endures."

You who are not Jewish (which I have been so poorly, but
which I am), I will introduce you to my land. You who are no
writer (which I have been so poorly, but which I am), I will
give you my books. You who are Jewish and, perhaps, a writer:
You will reproach me with losing the prey for the shadow.
And, in order to punish me, you will deny the validity of these
pages.
Have you seen how a word lives?
Have you seen how two words live?
Then listen.

I give you the word of my books.

(Of course, writing is complicated to deal with.
Words are touchy and unpredictable, but also ca-
pable of generosity and understanding.
    Meeting them, you must turn over a new leaf.
You must forget what you know to make room for
what you are going to learn.)

Look at the word and how it lives.
Look at words and how they live.
And then listen.

I give you the fate of my books,
which is the fate of Sarah and Yukel.

(All I wanted to do was tell of their tragic love.
But the space around them is alive with the signs
of their origin. Forgotten letters of the alphabet
slip in and mingle with the letters of their names,
their gestures, and their words so that I am no
longer sure where they are and where they are
not. Just as we never know where we are and
where we are not: so much is the world a part of
us.)

I give you the world of my books,
which is the world of Sarah and Yukel.

You have guessed that I prize highly what is said—even
more, perhaps than what is written. Because what is written
lacks my voice. And that is what I believe in. I mean the cre-
ative voice, not the voice which is merely an accessory and a
servant.
    Question me, you for whom I am speaking. Out of the si-

lence, where they are enshrined, I will draw the answers to
your questions. Are you satisfied? It is not I who answer. It is
the sentences.

*(Words rush in and knock everything over.
They want, each, to get their chance to convince.
The true human dialogue, that of hands and
eyes, is a silent dialogue. There is no such thing
(spoken or written) as a dialogue between per-
sons. So I ask myself, what is our part in a dis-
cussion or a tale. We are the instrument that
takes itself seriously. No doubt, in accepting our
words (up to a certain point) we sometimes suc-
ceed in identifying with them. Then we seem to
express the truth. But this happens only the moment we step aside, the moment we break with
our past and future in order to be the past and
future of the word, the moment we become the
silence of our five senses, polished copper plate
where we all judge ourselves (see ourselves
judged) in the merciless graph: whether we en-
grave our letters or paint them, whether our writing is porch and avenue or a trail blown by the
wind, whether we confided nothing or revealed
all. It is, finally, the moment we no longer have
faces that we may dare to show them.*

*"Calligraphy is one of the arts of living, and
the most aristocratic," noted Reb Debbora.*

*Happy those who take pains forming their let-
ters, whose words are meticulously drawn. They
sleep and wake up in palaces. The others are tor-
mented. Their world is formless, subject to thousands of interpretations, occasion for constant
metamorphoses. Under their pens, vowels are
like fish mouths on the hook, out of the water;
consonants like scales scraped off. They live
cramped in their deeds, in their hovels of ink.
The infinite haunts them and, alone, may save
them: as the grain of sand is saved if it succeeds
in becoming a star.)*

To be the world, the seasons, of soothed, reconciled words. To be the silence in their repose and above their bloody battles. For often words are bows, and utterances arrows, bright or dark. The sense of these wars? A decisive encounter where the losers, betrayed by their wounds, in falling describe the page of writing which the victors dedicate to the chosen who, unwittingly, launched it. In fact, the battle is fought in order to affirm the supremacy of word over man, and of word over word. The chosen are stretcher-bearers who complacently derive honor and glory from a task which exposes them only to relative danger.

And yet, the task is beautiful — beautiful like an adventuress in love with sincerity: to give life back to the wounded without history, to bring them back to the world of legends and history. For my tales, I need words with palpable wounds, words resuscitated, nursed back to life.

> I have so little time to dream.
> I have all the time in the world.
>
> I speak in my dream.
> I speak after my dreams.

"Yukel, tell us of silence which is the end and the beginning, being the soul of words,

just as singer and martyr are, at a given moment, the soul of the world."

"I will take you up to the door. You have the key."

5

A book without room for the world would be no book. It would lack the most beautiful pages, those on the left, in which even the smallest pebble is reflected.

One evening, on leaving the synagogue, Reb Noual said to Reb Seriel:

"The world is clear water in a china bowl. You may clutch the bowl in your hands, but you will never seize the clear water."

"I can dip my fingers in, or drink it," replied Reb Seriel.

"What for?" said Reb Noual then. "Your fingers would dry immediately, and your thirst be quenched but for a moment."

And he concluded:

"Thirst is our lot."

"Yukel, tell us of our miserable thirst."

"The five continents are the five fingers on the hand of Judaism.

"Each Jew on each continent knows the story of his finger,
the story of his right,
the nostalgic story of his right hand,
the story of his fist,
the story of the blood in his hand,
the story of his bleeding hand."

"For any citizen," wrote Reb Leda, "the fatherland is the everyday reality our eyes and feet encounter. It is the rock where soul and body are thrown and break."

And elsewhere:

"The story of my country rests on five steps. The story of my country is lit by five torches. To tell the story of my country, five waves stir up the sea. To weep over the story of my country, five clouds break into rain."

"Yukel, tell us of the wave and the torch, the step and the cloud."

"I will tell you the story of the olive tree which died of no longer recognizing the soil of my country.

"I will tell you the story of the date tree which died of being left on the threshold of my country.

"I will tell you the story of the donkey which died of no longer knowing the paths of my country.

"I will tell you the story of the dog which died of having lost its master."

"Yukel, tell us the story of your country."

"I have no country. I am Yukel Serafi. And my life is the story."

I could have been this man. I share his birth.

Being Jewish means having to justify your existence. It means having the same sleepless nights in common, suffering the same insults. It means desperately looking for the same buoy, the same helping hand. It means swimming, swimming, swimming in order not to sink.

Being Jewish means having the same rings under the eyes, the same sceptical smile — yet the Jew is capable of great enthusiasm. It means facing the forbidden sun and blinking.

A victim of injustice, the Jew is the enemy of those who base their justice on injustice. He is a target for those in absolute power, because embarrassing. Embarrassing, because refractory.

Being Jewish means learning to move a few yards from the ground your right to which is challenged. It means not knowing any more if the earth consists of water, or air, or oblivion.

What stratagems he uses to survive. How inventive his means, how diligent his metamorphoses.

Deduce. Adapt. Plan. He can be hounded, but not destroyed.

Half man, half fish, half bird, half ghost: there is always one half of him which escapes the hangman.

> ("*Look how his face turns into a bird,*" *said Reb Elfer to Reb Yod.* "*And how the squirrel tries to recognize itself in this face.*
>
> "*Look how his face turns into a branch. And how the branch blossoms for the face.*
>
> "*From the alder to the fir, from the abundant baobab to the delicate profile of the spindle tree: look how the world of trees ages and dies in man's face.*
>
> "*For us, too, the time of transparency will come.*")

Reb Sunai wrote: "Take a medlar. Offer half to your companion. After the medlar is eaten, the taste stays in the mouth, and friendship grows.

"The transparency of the object is beyond the object, in its ordained fullness.

"The transparency of man."

And Reb Isaac: "I am listening, son. And I see through you to the sky."

6

You gave birth to me because you could only
give me what you are.
   Mother, you gave birth to my death.
   Ever since, I live and die in you,
who are love.
   Ever since, I am reborn of our death.

"Yukel, will you tell us of the face?"

   ("All faces are His. Hence, He has no face."
                                    —Reb Alen

   "By and by, you lose your body. Because of the
night you walk into. Or because the light with-
draws. You lose your features. Smoothed out.
Then transparent.
   "You slide, cheek along cheek, forehead along
groin. You run parallel to your blood.
   "For, the face is only the frozen moment of the
rising oars or their dip into the sea."
                                    —Reb Zaccai

   "On the threshold of the seventh day, God
closed the envelope of the world, where the stars

gleamed. He closed it with his seal, which man
calls by the blinding name: sun."

—Reb Jais

"Will the fields of your writings satisfy our
hunger?" Reb Egor was asked by one of his dis-
ciples.
"The desire which is on this side of the word,"
Reb Egor answered, "is also on the other."
"If you were no longer hungry or thirsty, why
would I still write?")

A mother's portrait is the seal on the back of an envelope. It tells the price and protects the opening.

Each letter contains the inventory of a blade of wheat.

("You try to make my teaching look like yours.
But consider that each of my words is a prodigal
son I question," said Reb Stil.

And Reb Odar: "We are treated like imposters.
But surely we are the true rabbis. What we say is
not on record anywhere. Those who know how to
read us, read us in themselves. For within them,
our words are ordered as in the works of our
sages.")

"Faith comes at the end of reasoning," stated Reb Nahum. "You get there by instinct—or pushed by failure.

"In order to be heard, I ventured into the room where the rabbis confront one another. I have not left since.

"How could an argument soothe or settle a controversy, when every word is a nest for a bird of doubt?"

And Reb Mathias: "You found certainty in the woods of my doubt. So I carried a certainty which fled from me. And I am dying of uncertainty."

Hold your breath. Stop thinking for the time it takes to cross a river. There is order in the water running between the banks, the water which separates mud from mud, and palm from palm.

Cut your argument, your speech, so that silence may without fail play its ferryman's role.

Give the oars a chance, and the guide's hand.

If you open the envelope, do not harm the mother's face.
If you gather the rabbi's words, do not use them against him.
If you hope, watch how the trees breathe in our woods.

"Yukel, we left our frustrated shores behind and embarked on your book."

"You have not left the book since.

"You could not have.

"But sometimes the space between the lines is so large that you seem to tread on new ground.

"The margins are so wide."

The book chains us together.

7

Who could be less alone than a lonely man? All roads begin in him and have his heart as guiding star.
But between one star and another, there is the unfathomable refusal of silence.

I could have been this man, or someone like him.

"Yukel, tell us this man's story."
"I will tell you the story of his solitude."

To the blind man who begged for his blessing, Reb Yekel said:
"Speak to the man who sees with your missing eyes."

To the one-armed man who begged for his blessing, Reb Yekel said:
"Speak to the man who builds with your missing arm."

To the legless man who begged for his blessing, Reb Yekel said:
"Speak to the man who moves on your missing legs."

To the deaf-mute who begged for his blessing, Reb Yekel gave a bottle of oil so that his lamp might celebrate the night.

"Unless you have seen the men of my race in the synagogue," said Reb Yekel, "unless you have seen them cradling in their arms, like a child, the heavy scroll of their divine past in its casket of ornamental wood or velvet, with its four silver towers, unless you have seen them, in their silk-fringed shawls, sinking into themselves as into an abyss, unless you have heard their sobs turning into prayer, and their prayer into a song from beyond memory: you had better forego speaking of solitude."

When a man celebrates his God, he changes his sex. He becomes a season of the soul. And the soul is feminine.

"Prophets and monks always wear skirts."

Reb Yekel compared the Jew to a tile proffered and stomped on: "The man who has not heard a tile groan under the heels of indifferent passers had better forego speaking of solitude."

The strength of the tile is that it is stone. The Jews have taken shelter behind the stones thrown at them. Once returned to dust, they will be part of the stones thrown at their descendants. They know this. You cannot surprise them. They are spellbound by fate. Their strength is their faith in the stone: the stone that makes them bleed and the stone that shelters.

"When the waters parted," Reb Yekel taught, "they freed the stone. The stone, in turn, gave us our freedom. For only within our four walls are we really free."

And Reb Madoun: "Contrary to general opinion, solitude is no blindfold. It is an eye superbly conscious of being an eye, conscious that, in order to be, it must refuse all solicitation and pursue its bold and monstrous course."

Solitude kept watch in Reb Madoun's eyes, in Reb Yekel's eyes, as the death of a landscape keeps watch in the well. Therefore I know its features.

Solitude is hereditary. Siamese twins claim our soul. One brings forth death, the other life.

(*And he said to Reb Yekel:*
"*The believer, who hands the 'Sefer Torah' to his fellow worshipers to kiss, knows that, outside the Temple walls, perhaps even within, he must defend it like an unmarried mother the fruit of her guilty love. So they accuse us.*"

And he said to Reb Yekel:
"*The believer knows: if he lost his 'taleth' which covers him from head to loins, bridal veil whose train has been cut to avoid traces, he knows if he lost his shawl and his God (his God with his shawl) he would lose his reason to be, like a bride who lost her husband on the wedding day.*
"*So they weaken us.*"

And he said to Reb Yekel:
"*Once the service is over, like a piece of brocade with golden rosettas, rolled up again by the melancholy merchant of immortality, the believer knows he will find the old misery and night. So they kill us.*
"*But we know how to die naked.*"

And Reb Yekel said:
"*I am Yekel with his shadow. And the shadow is larger than I am.*
"*I carry all paths within me: the path of man and, hidden, the path of the stone.*
"*I carry you, brothers,*
"*like a bunch of keys.*")

8

God rests in man,
as man rests under a tree.
And the shadow, by grace of God, is man
in the tree, and tree in man.

I could have been this man. I have shared his shadow.
"Yukel, tell us of the shadow we have in common."

> *("A shadow is never more than a shadow," said*
> *Reb Hazel. But Ioakim Elia, who knew the origin*
> *of shadows, did not like this inference.*
> *"A shadow is never more than appearance," he*
> *said. "But we know that the world, each morn-*
> *ing, scuttles itself to make room for appearance."*
> *"But this world," replied Reb Hazel, "how can*
> *you grasp it, if it does not exist?"*
> *"I can grasp what I see," said Ioakim Elia. "I*
> *only have to open or close my eyes.")*

"Have you thought," said Reb Sia to his New Year's guests,
"of the importance of the shadow? It is reflection and the sacrifice of reflection. It is man's double and negation. It is also a
cool oasis.

"But do not confuse shadow with gutted light. For shadow is at the same time focus of light and dead language."

And the first guest answered:

"I have thought of it, thanks to you, master. I am now a shadow. I have kept my body. I have my eyes, my mouth. I hear my heart beat with my hand. And yet I hover, lighter than a feather. Is this not wonderful?"

And the second guest answered:

"I have thought of it, thanks to you, master. I know now that death is not the loss of memory, but its apotheosis. An apotheosis of light. You no longer need to make an effort to remember. You see all the way back to childhood. You are reduced to eye and ear, as at the theater. This makes me wonder: does the audience at these secular stage amusements know that a play is an apprenticeship and that, in those amusing, moving, or disconcerting hours, they learn, passively, to die."

And the third guest answered:

"I have thought of it, thanks to you, master. When, as a child, I passed you and one of your disciples in the street, I said to myself: 'It must be like this when shadows talk.' Your pallor, your frozen smile, your lack of vitality were the origin of all my thinking."

"What you took for lack of vitality is, on the contrary, vitality at its apex," Reb Sia replied. And he added:

"The man crazy about writing dreams of being a shadow in order to marry the water. From this union, books are born.

"But the shadow is only a spot of memory, perceived by the eye.

"Our memory of God (which grows as we keep His law) transforms the believer into an abundant fig tree known by the rustling of its leaves and its peculiar scent.

"The shadow is place and becoming of God on the implacable path of the light."

I could have been this shadow. I have shared its daring.

"Yukel, tell us the exploits of your shadow."

"I will tell you the story of Nathan Seichell."

In the ghetto, his name is revered. He lives among his
people like a fountain in a small square. He is quoted. He is
treated with familiarity and yet with deference. He is also
feared: people do not wish to displease him. The most beautiful room is for Nathan Seichell: an abandoned nook, fur-
nished by the imagination, most comfortable (so people are
persuaded). And on Passover? On Passover, he eats on silver
plates with engraved borders, borrowed from the Cohn family
which is, rightly, proud of them.

For some, Nathan is the sage outside time, the seer to consult. Women discuss him among themselves:

"And you know what Nathan said to me?"

"You will have a son who will drink at the breast of night.
He will grow like an olive tree watered by your tears."

"Will my son not be born from my womb? You worry me,
Nathan. Why will I cry so much?"

"And you know what he said?"

"Your son will be your shadow."

"Then I will rest at my son's feet."

"And you know what he said?"

"You will wallow in pain."

"But I will have had my joy."

"And you know what he said?"

"Joy, in the ghetto, is a candle. Hope, a conflagration."

Frightening, sometimes, as the Kabbalists were. — But he
owes them nothing.

"At the origin, there is language. God is a circle of luminous
letters. He is each of the letters of His Name. He is also the
middle, the void of the circle where man and the woman about
to be mother stand.

"Confronted with one of the divine letters — the circle bro-
ken — the creature recognized by its own sign will bear its
mark."

"You believe in chance, Nathan?"

"Chance is the explanation people give to those unforeseen
encounters which upset their lives. Chance is no business of

God's. He does not try to explain. Adonai is. And everything is, in its hour, around Him, through Him.

"Thus, we know only a part of Adonai, the part which appeared to us in a steady flash of lightning. — In movement, His name, like Himself, is rebellious light.

"Thus, we know only a part of our Lord. It gives us access to the All beyond knowledge.

"Our life, in its good aspects, has the form of a revealed letter. The sounds which gave birth to it reverberate within us.

"Our life, in its evil aspects, has the form of an upside down letter, excluded from the Book of Books because it is illegible."

And Nathan added further:

"Aie . . . Aie . . . The groans of the Jewish people are in the body of the Eternal."

For others, Nathan is the disinterested companion who puts his experience at the disposal of the community.

"Who gave you this advice?"

"Nathan."

Nothing is begun without his approval. If he turns out to be wrong, he was misunderstood.

At any reunion, he is the guest of honor. And in the synagogue (the walls of the humblest synagogue are immense pieces of sky) his voice drowns out the voice of whole worlds.

"Mommy, tell me about Nathan Seichell."

Every child wants to drink his mother's words of truth. And the mother perpetuates the legends.

"Boys," she says, "always have a thousand tricks up their sleeves. But Nathan was different. Not that he was above games. He just never seemed altogether present."

"Nathan, you are so absent-minded it will ruin you."

"It saves me," he replied. "It will save us all."

"Look here," his uncle David countered. "Since when does one defend one's interests by turning one's back?"

One morning, a little before noon, his older sister had gone to meet him as she did every day, when she suddenly saw him appear in the light in front of her. (She was so startled she froze on the spot). She saw him wave at her before disappearing: first one arm, then the other, the legs then, and finally the face, as if between two ocean waves. But he did not seem to struggle. — Was she in the street? Was she living a nightmare? She tried to cry for help, but her voice had no sound, it was stretched out under her. She waited, helpless, to get it back, waited for someone to help her voice pull itself together and give it back to her. In vain. Her heart carried her off toward the open sea. She knew she would never again reach port.

"Nathan, you are so absent-minded it will cost you your life."

Immediately after, a rumor spread through the ghetto that Nathan, son of Rachel, had drowned in his soul (his clothes bore witness on the spot where they had been left) and that his sister was rocked by the waves, just as the faithful in prayer seem to be standing, but are really on their backs.

> (We think they are standing because we cannot imagine them otherwise. With their shawls around their shoulders they are, in fact, boats at the mercy of wind and sea. At the hours of service the waves come, sometimes so big they shake the synagogue. Leaving the synagogue is a real landing. You return to your street, your family, as after a rewarding absence.)

"I knew it would happen," screamed his uncle David. "Now Nathan is walking around naked."

But all the others around uncle David begged:

"Nathan, Nathan, show yourself."

"Are you here, there?"

"Are you before, behind us?"

"Are you up there?"

"Are you down beneath?"

"We all have been lost in ourselves, but the others could see and touch us."

"Nathan, let us see you, and we will lead you back to the earth."

At that point, a voice was heard. Indistinct at first (miracles are not reassuring the moment they happen), then clearer and clearer as they got used to it (to get used to a miracle means forgetting it—hence, everything is a miracle). A voice of flesh and sparkling scales. A voice was seen exhibiting its words:

"I am luminous like the dialogue of the seven-armed candelabra in the synagogue, on both sides of the chest with the parchments of the Law about which a poet said that, unrolled, they are the shores of the kingdom of God. But I am shadow, crest and abyss of shadow."

The crowd was getting larger and more excited. They begged:

"Let us see you, Nathan."

"Let us see you."

The voice went on:

"I am what solicits and separates, limits and unfolds. I am the second presence."

People were so worked up that it worried the outsiders. Alerted soldiers entered the ghetto, weapon in hand, to reestablish order. The agitators would be judged and punished. Seichell's older sister would be the first to be dragged by her hair before the tribunal.—But who could catch her in the middle of the ocean?

As the soldiers attacked the protesting crowd with increasing violence, the following happened: pushed back without knowing how or by whom, kept apart from their victims just when they thought of striking, they hit the empty air with their sabres. And the emptiness spread and settled among them. The soldiers were blinded with flowing blood, but not a single ghetto dweller was hurt. The empty air bled. Also the soldiers: they could not avoid their own swords.

The ghetto was like an island, its outline defined, through the arm of Nathan Seichell, by the inhabitants' anger, stubbornness, faith, and love.

"This is the story," concluded the mother.

Men of my race develop in a cocoon. They are locked inside their fears and convictions. They belong to the family of silkworms (night silkworms) and of fish, whose cocoon is the ocean.

Every Jew drags behind himself a scrap of the ghetto, a scrap of rescued land where he takes refuge when alarmed. His chains isolate him from the world. But the chains fall when Jews are among themselves.

Cursed land, received like the promised land. Solitary land — semblance of a land — with the color of hope.

Lavish absence.

> *("Events half open for us the door of a gallery of mirrors where we see ourselves at all ages. They show within us long halls of idealized and occasional portraits.*
>
> *"We draw courage from their example," said Reb Silon.*
>
> *"Look at these people," said Reb Mathias. "They are wells chased away from their water. When their step gets heavier, they have recaptured their land.")*

9

*(The sleeping quarters of screams stretch be-
yond echo's reach. Formerly, one only heard
screams when they awoke. And it happened that
they slept a long time. Nowadays, they no longer
sleep at all.*

*One day, before he died, the shaved rabbi who,
in his deportation clothes, no longer looked like a
rabbi, said to me:*
*"What is the water in a lake? A blank page.
The ripples are its wrinkles. And every one is a
wound.*
*"A lake without ripples is a mirror. A wrinkled
lake is a face.*
"In their markings, our faces reflect God's."

I turned to the rabbi and answered:
*"You lie. What about the face of the in-
nocent?"*

The rabbi turned to me and explained:
*"The wrinkles of the innocent are ripples a
breeze sketches and undoes as it subsides.*
"Wonder is a twinkle of the skin.
"God is in the slightest shiver."

I turned to the rabbi and said:
*"God is in the wind, Rabbi, in the wind which
wreaks havoc."*

And the rabbi interrupted me:
"Do not blaspheme, Yukel. If the tree is a tree,
it is because it has never blasphemed. Each of its
knots is a bond.")

So we are brothers in our faces.

Here, elsewhere; elsewhere, here: a glass block, a ball.

The globe is pulverized by its reflections. In the sun, you can admire their variety. All the fond shades of men — and of the things enumerated in their eyes. There are blue and red reflections. There is the yellow reflection, the green. The yellow will never turn blue, nor the green red.

"Our breast is a jail," wrote Reb Veda. "Our ribs are the bars which keep us from suffocating.

"You will live in your jail, brother, for your salvation. The elect is a prisoner of the transmitted word of God. For its survival, he makes his body into a cell fitting the word.

"You will know the happiness of being inhabited by your God."

To which Reb Sia replied:

"The happiness to be oneself is what the horse feels when it has thrown off its rider.

"But the earth I tread is infested with snakes. Accept me, Lord, as your mount. And let us together run across the starry infinite which unfolds through you."

10

*Before and after the word comes the sign
and, in the sign, the void where we grow.
Only the sign can be seen, being a wound.
But the eyes lie.*

I could have been this man. I have shared his love.

"Yukel, tell us about this man who could have been you."
"I will first tell you about the lie."

Reb Jacob, who was my first teacher, believed in the virtue of the lie because, so he said, there is no writing without lie. And writing is the way of God.

Reb Jacob also believed in eloquence. He compared it to a stone tearing the surface of a lake and to its misleading rings. The wound closes right up again. But the rings multiply and grow and bear witness — oh mockery — to the intensity of the pain.

The divine utterance is silenced as soon as it is pronounced. But we cling to its resonant rings, our inspired words.

Eloquence is created by the absence of a divine word.

It is at the beginning of speech. We are crushed by the deity. The echo dies as the voice weakens. The murmur is truly human.

Pomp and solemnity are the language of princes. They are

the lies of men. (Likewise lovers' caresses.) Nakedness, pov-
erty are the lies of God.

I will tell you about the lie of the rose, the fire contained in
its petals. (The rose is the most feminine of flowers.) I will tell
you about the number "3" whose symbol it is. The petals, two
at a time, suggest the shape of the "3." The corolla and stem
form a "9," which is three times three couples of petals. The
hand which plucks the rose and lifts it to the mouth traces,
unawares, the voluptuous progress of the number "3."

*(Why is the rose the symbol of the number "3?"
The narcissus, for example, with its mirror
shadow, the anemone regina or the ever green
iberis sempervirens with their petals like pairs of
butterflies, or even the flower commonly called
chickweed: all of them have more claim to this
honor.*

But the rose is the best liar.)

"Three times," said Reb Grisha, "once every three months,
the child in the womb kicks against the number "One,"
which is the first letter and which, added to itself (the mascu-
line "One," plus the feminine "One," plus the masculine-
feminine "One") forms the number "Three." "Three" pre-
sides over our fate.

"Man, who is at the same time *being, non-being, and super-
being*, incarnates it even beyond death."

And Reb Chemtob:

"The one is celebrated three times. For the One and Only is
shadow, half-light, and sun."

And Reb Liatob:

"The first letter torments the alphabet. For it is three times
itself and three times the letters it introduces."

I will tell you about the lie of big numbers and little numbers, the lie of circle and triangle, which are the passages and
impasse of sorcery.

I will tell you about the lie of faith which is consumed by flames, which does not lift you, but goes up in smoke.

> (*"The believer's heart,"* wrote *Reb Himsa, "is a stake where he sacrifices himself to the human vision of God."*
> And *Reb Loria: "Ashes, ashes, you are the believer's blood."*)

I will tell you about the third day.

I could have been this man. I have shared his days.

"Yukel, tell us about this man who is a lie in God."
"I will tell you about the price he paid for lying, that is to say, for living."

11

I learned to love men in the hour when I tried, with all my strength, to be loved.
This way the Jews love the Jews.
I learned to be a man.
I learned to speak pompously about man.
This way the Jews speak about Jews.
One day, my words became strangers to me and I fell silent.

("The story of my soul is that of the letters of the alphabet. Their shape let my senses perceive their advance across time and space towards their union in the word, at the foreseen hour and place of my birth.

"Two men are never at the same distance from language. For we develop differently in those regions of heart and mind which words embrace. We may be close to the truth of the word, or far from it. It is a question of having followed it in passing, or of having left everything in order to catch it.

"The word is virgin. I have watched it wake.

"The story of my soul is the story of my passionate quest of the word where the world is the price of my thought."

          —Reb Gaon

"Nobody can destroy a candle," said Reb Berre, "because it is the light of the soul."

To which Reb Bor replied that he put one out every night.

"If you blind a man," said Reb Berre, then, "does that mean you deprive his soul of the sun? The world inside is a black world. Each avowal, each gesture, is a candle which burns and, while we sleep, wakes deep within us.")

"Death is a woman who embroiders," wrote Reb Sohemi. "Her subjects are well known. But she surprises us with the color of her threads. This is why we are always astonished in her presence.

"An intricate canvas is our last bed."

("Our words do not join one another. Your hand is deaf, your eye blind."

—Reb Isel

"The soul can be compared to a mountain of silence lifted up by the word. One weak muscle, and it topples."

—Reb Diba)

"You believe in reason as if it were reasonable."

—Reb Son

"You read in my palms, you write in my eyes."

—Reb Sem

"You have to be mad to accept death, and wise to resign yourself to living."

—Reb Atem

"You are dead. You escape the imagination."

—Reb Zien

"A light in death, and there is life to be consumed."

—Reb Evi

I will tell you how being burrows various passages through the night of dreams towards the word.

There is, first of all, this hardly visible trace from letter to letter, from shadow to lighter shadow. Then this already conscious break-through of the word. Finally, the paved road of discourse and mastered writing.

But do not believe that madness has ever left us. Like pain, it lies in wait for us at each stage, I mean each time we run up against the word hidden in the word, the being buried in the being.

Alas that we cannot brush against insanity without the risk of losing our reason for good.

Madness and wisdom are the two poles of the day. Their future differs. For dawn, noon is the master. For dusk, midnight the desired beloved.

"I do not know," said Reb Arout, "if it is the break of day which is the height of madness, or if it is nightfall. I do not know if madness is wisdom, or if wisdom is the highest degree of madness."

Dusk plunges into the blazing world of abysses with their incandescent lakes. Dawn opens up with busy light and trusts the earth to the earth. Dusk watches over the roots. Dawn forms with the fruit.

Reb Arout said also: "Wisdom and madness are gifts of the same tree. But it stands among so many similar trees that man rarely encounters it. So he can eat without danger."

The wise and the mad (is it chance which decides?) are

pushed by a deep dissatisfaction towards the hidden branches. They let themselves be destroyed.

Madness has taken the face of lightning, wisdom that of a statue. They cause enthusiasm among ants — while above the subjugated regions, crowned eagles puncture their blue kingdom.

A Jew and a Jewess (out of the thousands and millions) lost their forehead and shoulders, became numb legs, skinnier from day to day. On their way, there was not a single friend, only walls they could not lean against.

"Look," said Abel. "We have a wall left. And we deafen it with our sighs."

And Tima: "Silence lives in the stone. Our pains will petrify when our gestures no longer make sense. But our tears, brothers, who will take them on himself?"

There were walls which separated them from people.

12

Night does away with colors. It lets blaze the color of the soul.

"The number '4,' " he said, "is the number of our ruin. Do not think I am mad. The number '4' equals 2 times 2. It is in the name of such obsolete logic that we are persecuted. For we hold that 2 times 2 equals also 5, or 7, or 9. You only need to consult the commentaries of our sages to verify. Not everything is simple in simplicity. We are hated because we do not enter into the simple calculations of mathematics.

"They were taught that 2+2=4. And they immediately deduced that we are superfluous.

"Take their latest invention, the swastika. Is it not the shadow of two joined '4's on our shrouds?

"We die so that the number '4' may reign twice, over men and over plants.

"A pebble on our graves. Chrysanthemums for those who pass away in peace."

(*Are we possibly the denial of the irrefutable proof that 2 plus 2 equals 4?*

"*We once were this proof. And they used it against us.*"

"*How, Yukel, how?*"

"In the name of Good and Evil, in the name of Heaven and Hell,

"in the name of the curve of the earth.

"For we are the torment of logic. In the addition of even numbers, we are the order and disorder of the uneven figure.")

13

We are given as pasture to the iron monster, to each link of the chain, to each brazen mouth. It sacrifices us to our steps.

What remains of a man's life? Not even the trace of his heel.

The word which takes over the watch covers its tracks because it obeys the laws of writing.

This way, any statement, any account, is but an adventure across the real and the imaginary, across life and the dream of life, adventure of a pen in pursuit of itself.

(In town, a man walks on the water of street-lamps and the moon.

A man (the same?) writes, and each of his steps is a word on the bright page.

A man, obsessed, who does not know how to express himself.

A man hard pressed.

—His image.)

They have the hollow cheeks of Reb Daber whose face, it was said, kept the imprint of the left and right forefingers of God's messenger who interrupted the rabbi's prayer to kiss his forehead.

Heirs of Reb Daber's hollow cheeks, what has become of

the fingerprints of God's messenger on their faces, of the kiss on their foreheads bathed in prayer?

They have the thin lips of Reb Antar who, it was said, had so often pronounced the name of God that his worn mouth no longer had the shape of flesh.

Heirs of Reb Antar's thin lips, what have they done with the venerated name of God which ate away their mouths?

They have Reb Missah's high forehead which, it was said, contained the egg from which, one day, the kingdom of Israel would spring, hatched by the warm wings of gratitude.

Heirs of Reb Missah's high forehead, what have they done with the warm wings of gratitude and with the egg from which, one day, the kingdom of Israel will spring?

They have the pen-stroke eyes of Reb Ezard who, it was said, had so often erased his writings that nothing remains of his works but the rallied name of God.

Heirs of Reb Ezard's eyes, what have they done with the glorious name which dazzled them, and with the lesson about unworthy writing?

They have the hooked nose of Reb Ephrat who, it was said, in chanting inhaled the roses of dawn and sand, of which he made, at night, a bouquet of hope and love.

Heirs of Reb Ephrat's hooked nose, what have they done with the bouquet of hope and love?

Their features define them, precede them, imprison them.

But who is responsible for his features?

A drop of blood sealed their lips. The earth suddenly seemed a madwoman in a red polka dot dress, her gestures hallucinatory weddings of ashes.

An owl was the frightful soul of this place.

Elsewhere, far away, among the clouds, the dead they evoke are gathered. They sit around a wooden table. They sit on chairs of wood and wicker. Elsewhere, on the other side of day, there are the dead, their future masters, in care of the dark.

A sage: We, the witnesses, judged and sentenced so that we would forget our impotence and spend our time drilling the avenue of our death as we had, formerly, in our respective countries, the royal road of our breath . . .

A sage: We, sages, we, the witnesses . . .

A sage: Fallen capitals in the center of the world, small provinces, humble villages: all our stones, faithful birds, have followed us here.

And we repeat the words of our childhood and of our old age. One cannot escape images.

A sage: We, inhabitants and ghosts . . .

A sage: . . . for the flesh is eternal, mother of laughter and pain . . .

A sage: . . . for the soul we come from had no purpose but to ripen the hand, as sun and water ripen the manifold gifts of the tree . . .

A sage: The soul we are going to is snow country . . .

A sage: . . . country cut out of water hardened by the cold. The water keeps us. So do the glaciers, eyes grown large of those who disappeared.

A sage: Where the eye can still rest, where the ear can still hear, where the nose can still smell, where the fingers can still touch, rises a wall.

A sage: To build walls, is that not living?

A sage: Strange that we should meet at a definite moment when, for centuries, we had not made any difference between night and day. And how do we know the hour? We must have rethought time, and must have been aware of forging ourselves new ties. But did we not do so to cheat boredom? We could as well not have met. (We wanted nothing more than to establish ties.) Strange. We have met.

A sage: We calculated the distance between us. We stopped dying.

A sage: Death is absence in itself and in space.

A sage: Are we the echo whose voice centuries could not ᵒ stifle?

A sage: Are we the last gasp of oblivion?

A sage: A man is riveted to all he has approached, to all he has been taught.
Riveted.

A sage: I wanted to stop dying.

A sage: We sought each other.

A sage: We wanted to stop dying.

A sage: A stone
    and higher up
    a stone.

A sage: A door
    and higher up
    a door.

A sage: A window
    and higher up
    a window.

A sage: The grass
            and higher up
            the flower.

A sage: The trunk
            and higher up
            the branches.

A sage: The knee
            and higher up
            the shoulder.

A sage: The neck
            and higher up
            the eyes.

A sage: We wanted to rise without return.

A sage: We helped one another.

A sage: Will we destroy the stone to reach the stone?

A sage: Will we destroy the door to reach the door?

A sage: Will we destroy the window to reach the window?

A sage: Will we trample the grass to reach the flower?

A sage: Will we fell the tree to reach the branches?

A sage: Will we break the knee to reach the shoulder?

A sage: Will we break the neck to reach the eyes?

A sage: Death is the monotonous ascent of death.

A sage: We will destroy the stone to reach the door.

A sage: Do we have to?

A sage: We will destroy the door to reach the window.

A sage: Do we have to?

A sage: We will destroy the window to reach the window.

A sage: Do we have to?

A sage: We will trample the grass to reach the branches.

A sage: Do we have to?

A sage: We will break the knees to reach the eyes.

A sage: Do we have to?

A sage: We will destroy ourselves in the landscape.

A sage: Do we have to?

A sage: We will destroy ourselves in men.

A sage: Do we have to?

A sage: We will destroy ourselves in things.

A sage: Do we have to?

A sage: We will destroy ourselves in death.

"Look, Yukel," said Sarah, "look at the sky blossoming in its clouds."

Reb Elam, who preached renunciation, wrote this:

> "I blossom in my death.
> Impregnable flower.
> Not knowing where it is
> you cannot smell it.
> But you know it exists.
> So you go in search.
> You will die without finding:
> it is also your death."

"The Israelite," he wrote further, "has his eyes turned toward Jerusalem in the way the grown child looks at his mother's womb: the cause of his misfortunes.

"Alas, Jerusalem is buried under the ruins of the Temple. And the womb is responsible, it continues to expel eyes fascinated by the giant crystals of the void.

"The salvation of the Jewish people lies in severance, in solidarity at the heart of severance."

But Reb Léoum, the rabbi most listened to, answered him:

"The salvation of the Jewish people lies in surviving the bitter herbs which cover our fields of patience."

One was crazy about death, the other about life.

The Jewish world begins with us, with our first steps in the world.

The Jewish world is based on written law, on a logic of words one cannot deny.

So the country of the Jews is on the scale of their world, because it is a book.

Every Jew lives within a personified word which allows him to enter into all written words.

Every Jew lives in a key-word, a word of pain, a password, which the rabbis comment on.

The Jew's fatherland is a sacred text amid the commentaries it has given rise to.

Hence, every Jew is in the Law.

Hence, every Jew makes the Law.

Hence, the Law is Jewish.

"You can free yourself of an object, of a face, of an obsession," said Reb Samuel. "You cannot free yourself of a word. The word is your birth and your death."

("*Day is start, night beginning. Thus innocence is born.*"

— Reb Fahim

"*You are beautiful with all my reasons for finding you beautiful, which you call my unreason.*"

— Reb Boaz)

The Book of the Absent

Second Part

"You are like," said Reb Eglon, "a branch hanging over a torrent, trying to hold back the water. Is it effort which bends it, or tiredness?"

"I am tired," answered Reb Aloun. "And all my energy is in my tiredness."

"In that case," continued Reb Eglon, "you are like the pages of my collections, whose effort to contain thought fuses with blank allegiance to the hand which turns them."

1

*She has loved all, excused all, given all. She is
our law, and we watch over her.*

— Reb Coldré

The road I have taken is the roughest. The longest. The
most daring.

It begins with difficulty (the difficulty of being and writing)
and ends with difficulty.

*("Difficulty is self-contained," said Reb Akad.
"It cannot be resolved, except by another difficulty we have to face."*

*And Reb Lissah: "Difficulty continues to live
in us by marrying a difficulty of the opposite sex.
It always engenders legitimate difficulties.")*

"Pain and joy are a terrible couple," said Reb Lernia. "In all
joy, there is a lake of bitterness; in all pain, a corner of a garden of joy.

"But misfortune is straighter than the date tree and more fa-
tal than the arrow."

And Reb Leir: "Misfortune saves and breaks us. It is the key
we have inherited."

("Why, my God," wrote Reb Doubré, "why force us to turn to You, to pierce our walls, when You are everywhere?"

This was doubtless what Reb Tal had in mind when he noted: "Once in the book, we must use the key which words have forged for us, and which we must discover.

"Without it, we run against a locked door on each page.")

The road I have taken is the one laid out by the people of my race: the road of intelligence and instinct (instinct before intelligence, and intelligence against instinct), the road of controversy and doubt. But at the end of it there is salvation—which is another doubt.

"And God," said Reb Daber, "is He not the island where the Jew lands and finds his brothers, who ask him about his voyage? Each second spent on the sea is a pact with the wave.

"Thanks to you, the ocean breaks on this lonely beach."

The wave is the male expression of the repetitive history of a people absorbed in itself.

"Come in with your words," said Reb Emat. "Today, it is they that are giving the feast."

And Reb Aria: "When the sky is serene, the waves rock like the Jews in prayer. For the sky of the synagogue is pure like a summer morning."

The Jew floats on words learned in the sun.

"If you sometimes think that God does not see you," wrote Reb Servi, "it is because He has humbled Himself to the point where you confuse Him with the fly which buzzes on your

window pane. But this proves his omnipotence: He is, at the same time, All and Nothing—
  glorious spirit and hair beneath notice."

"This conversation around a book warms me more than a glass of wine," said Reb Acher. "With you, I drink at the sources of my soul. Like beings, books have their share of fortune."

"You spoke, master," said Reb Eskel, "and we listened to you in the order of your teaching. But is it not inscribed in a universe of disorder, like the raging sea is for the boat which cleaves it?"

"The word is a horse. Its gallop whirls up the dust on the road. It forces the passers-by to lower their eyes."

"Your words have become our mounts, master," said Reb Lindel. "But we have not gone far. We went in circles, as in the circus. No doubt, we are wretched horsemen?"

"The tree goes in rings to its full height, and the bee around its honey-probe. Did not Reb Azar write: 'The road of knowledge is rounder than an apple?'"

2

It is not that one wants to be free. But one dreams of it.

("You lean on water, and are surprised that you sink."
                                        —Reb Hamel

"Do not confuse justice and truth. Justice is done in the name of truth. And truth remains to be found."
                                        —Reb Agam

"You have often been wrong. You are just."
                                        —Reb Ares)

"He is my enemy, and I did not know him.
                                        —Reb Elal

"He is unjust toward me, you are just to me. I am without defense."
                                        —Reb Mordoh

Yukel, you come from the heart of the ages, and the heart of the ages is a bit like a cloud.

You come from the sea which cut you off from yourself, cut

you off from your shadow and your light, your stone and your
grass,

cut you off without pity.

Your youth sleeps in the lakes of the book. It is fragile like
liquid shadows. Like the male and female shadows stretched
side by side who, through their love, across the centuries,
have become the cursed couple of the lake.

You still have the earth.

The road: a door in reach.

And you open it with a look so disfigured that it cannot go
far, a look which drags itself.

And you open it with a heart so worn that it cannot support
you long.

And you open it with a key so rusty that it has trouble enter-
ing the lock. And the lock is also rusty.

The walls pursue the one who left them.

You were the palm tree which gave shadow to the walls.

> ("We are living in a foreign country," said Reb
> Dambah, "where the Sabbath is kept only in our
> hearts. Ah, when will our heartbeat be one with
> that of the city?"
> And Reb Mendel: "We live in the open fan of
> our voices in the void.")

The book is the blank space of sleep. You sleep standing up,
and the world rounds itself without you. A world which will
weigh on your shoulders with all its years of laughter and
tears, which you will face on waking up.

"You fulfil yourself, my son," said Reb Safer, "with your lost
riches which led you to conquer yourself. You have nothing
left. You are finally a man in the image of God. For God, who
is without possessions, is richness for all."

Yukel, you are the fortune of the world, and you are naked.

You are covered with blood. And your hangmen protest
their innocence.

Your hangmen have your voice and your hands.

"They want to kill us off," said Reb Bender.

"To crush our foreheads, they have their foreheads hardened with hate.

"To drown our eyes, they have their eyes flooded with hate.

"To subdue our mouths, they have their mouths full of hate.

"To stifle our chests, they have their chests inflated with hate.

"To bend our knees, they have their knees oiled with hate.

"For only a human body can destroy the harmonious body of man in its chances and recesses of flesh and skin."

And Reb Dolé: "They wound us deeply. Their red-hot iron is a sixth finger on their hand."

Yukel, you are alone in the world, and the world steps aside when you pass.

"It is not the diamond they give wide berth," said Reb Nebil, "but the abyss whose body we are.

"As for our soul, who will ever know how it shines in that depth?"

You are the cruelest of your hangmen.

You are the Jewish hangman among the others.

To crush your forehead, you have a forehead haunted by love.

To drown your eyes, you have eyes flooded with love.

To subdue your mouth, you have a mouth full of love.

To stifle your chest, you have a chest inflated with love.

To smash your fingers, you have fingers counted by love.

To bend your knees, you have knees oiled with love.

"The love we feel for our people," said Reb Taer, "is more painful than the blows from our enemies. Each time one of our brothers dies, we die his death with him."

And Reb Levit: "You are at the mercy of your soul in love with its source. You die of an impossible love which revives with each new day."

The dream of the sea is eternal. So is the dream of Israel.

"We are dreamers kept asleep," said Reb Tiane. "But even if we are awakened some day, our dream will not be over."

You are asleep, Yukel, with your palm on the cover of your book.

The book closed.

"Who woke me," wrote Reb Chemtob, "from my ancestral sleep? Who touched my shoulder, kissed my forehead? Who put her head on my shoulder and took my hand? Who walked in step with me? Ah, who kept me from her bed in order to lead me to it? Who led me astray from my path?

"Woman, could your power be greater than God's?"

But Reb Josua answered him: "The man who walks in the desert dreams of an oasis. If God gave us thirst, he also gave us water. If he showed us the road, he also promised us rest."

Sarah, they have hounded you and all of us to such a point, cut down so many trees, drained so much water in us, that our desert is everywhere,

that, in the hollow of throat and belly, in the hollow of eyes and hands, you are my desert, and I yours.

> ("*What I call desert is dead life, a life on the model of the grain of sand.*"
> — Reb Nevi)

"Pick up some sand," wrote Reb Ivri, "and let it glide between your fingers. Then you will know the vanity of words.

"Sand is only sand, and the word, the struck flag of the word."

And elsewhere: "Can you swear that the grains of sand you pressed in your hand are the same which ran over your knee? They have become a thousand others which you did not know.

"So it is with your words, once they have been unleashed in the world filled with words."

Mother, I know you by the sweetness of your voice. Woods and valleys are not as good as our stubble fields where our hearts express themselves better. Pain needs a landscape of pain. Hence the world is ours. It is on our scale.

We are free in misfortune.

Give a twin rose to the rose, to the grain of sand another grain to show it off.

Mother, your lament seems cruel only amid roses. In the desert, it is older than the wind. The nomad knows it by the color the sand suddenly takes on hearing its song.

We must rejoin the first scream of our people, just as the sand must again find the first grain assailed by the sea.

Freedom consists in going back to the sources.

> *(That night, for no reason, the city classified its recollections, and every citizen had a right to pen and paper to write the history of the town.*
> *How the other people seemed at ease.*
> *While I strayed without memories. With shards of words, I rebuilt a destroyed city, where my books lay buried with broken bees' wings.)*

Yukel, that evening I could not stand my room any more than you yours. Did I know beforehand that I would run into you at the corner of my street? I walked straight ahead. You came to meet me. Without surprise, we walked side by side. The same desire of freedom made us feel close. We needed hardly an occasional glance to assure us we were near each other. I tried to make myself a soul out of yours, tried to climb without weakening the rungs of your suffering. I prepared myself to take on the ties you had felt. Each of them awakened a word. They gave me back my face. (In my writing, I am more nameless than a sheet in the wind, more transparent than a window pane). In order to be free, I had to have a face, you had to lose yours.

"Freedom," said Reb Aloum, "is the quickening conquest of oneself in an order as rigorous as that of oars in the water and of the hours on the thread of time."

Freedom is also the death of a face.

("*If freedom has wings,*" taught Reb Idrash,
"*it also has eyes, a forehead, genitals. Each time
it takes wing, it transfigures a bit of both the
world and man in the excitement of its
flowering.*"

And Reb Lima: "*In the beginning, freedom
was ten times engraved on the tables of the Law.
But we so little deserved it that the Prophet
broke them in his anger.*"

"*Any coercion is a ferment of freedom,*" Reb
Idrash taught further. "*How can you hope to be
free if you are not* bound *with all your blood to
your God and to man?*"

And Reb Lima: "*Freedom awakens gradually
as we become conscious of our ties, like the
sleeper of his senses. Then, finally, our actions
have a name.*"

A teaching which Reb Zalé translated into this
image: "*You think it is the bird which is free.
Wrong: it is the flower.*"

And Reb Elat into this motto: "*Love your ties
to their last splendor, and you will be free.*")

3

The Jew answers every question with another question.

—Reb Léma

My name is a question. It is also my freedom within my tendency to question.

—Reb Eglal

"Our hope is for knowledge," said Reb Mendel. But not all his disciples were of this opinion.

"We first have to agree on the sense you give to the word 'knowledge,' " said the oldest of them.

"Knowledge means questioning," answered Reb Mendel.

"What will we get out of these questions? What will we get out of all the answers which only lead to more questions, since questions are born of unsatisfactory answers?" asked the second disciple.

"The promise of a new question," replied Reb Mendel.

"There will be a moment," the oldest disciple continued, "when we have to stop interrogating. Either because there will be no answer possible, or because we will not be able to formulate any further questions. So why should we begin?"

"You see," said Reb Mendel: "at the end of an argument, there is always a decisive question unsettled."

"Questioning means taking the road to despair," continued

the second disciple. "We will never know what we are trying to learn."

"True knowledge is daily awareness that, in the end, one learns nothing. The Nothing is also knowledge, being the reverse of the All, as the air is the reverse of the wing."

"Our hope is the wings of despair. For how would we progress otherwise?" replied Reb Mendel.

"Intelligence," said the third disciple, "is more dangerous than the heart, which relies only on its own beat. Who among us can assert that he is right?"

"Only the hope to be right is real. Truth is the void," replied Reb Mendel.

"If the truth which is in man is void," continued the oldest disciple, "we are nothing in a body of flesh and skin. Therefore God, who is our truth, is also nothing?"

"God is a question," replied Reb Mendel. "A question which leads us to Him who is Light through and for us, who are nothing."

Our meeting, this evening, is about to end. The story I promised you is in your memory. Our passage across pact and imposture, across soul and hands without echo, has led us, via telling detours, to our eyes. They will understand and judge what they see in terms of what they have seen. Both truth and justice are incorruptible eyes: the innocent eyes of the child.

They see freedom in the distance.

The Book of the Absent

Third Part

1

> *"Where are you going?"*
> *"To the well of my childhood. And the way*
> *there is death."*
>
> — Reb Segré

"Yukel, you have not told us the story of the olive tree which died of no longer finding the soil of our country. You have not told us the story of the date tree which died of being left at the threshold of our country. You have not told us the story of the donkey which died of no longer walking the paths of our country. You have not told us the story of the dog which died of having lost his master.

"You have not told us the story of man.

"Yukel, you talked about the desert, and we looked for the date tree. You talked about Nathan Seichell, and we looked for the olive tree. You talked about wisdom and madness, and we looked for the donkey. You talked about life and death, and we looked for the dog.

"You have not told us the story of man."

"I talked to you about man's health. I talked to you about man's solitude and his lie. I talked to you about the proof of man's existence: God.

"I talked to you about the eloquence and nudity of the word."

"You talked to us about the word, and we looked for refuge in your words.

"We remember your words.

"You talked to us about freedom, which is a plant, and about the difficulty of being Jewish. You brought in the sayings of rabbis."

"I brought you my words. I talked to you about the difficulty of being Jewish, which is the same as the difficulty of writing. For Judaism and writing are but the same waiting, the same hope, the same wearing out."

"You hardly talked about Sarah and Yukel."

"It is the whole truth I wanted to express. And truth is a scream, a stubborn, ineradicable image which pulls us out of our torpor. An image which overwhelms or nauseates us.

"The fear of lying is the writer's honor. For he is called to bear witness and to build on his testimony.

"I have seen evil. In order to destroy it, I must be allowed to curse."

"You may curse, Yukel. You may."

"Reb Imar was asked if the sparrow's wings beat faster than the eagle's. He answered: 'My country is now a sparrow, now an eagle. Look, how sad I am to be doubly far from my country.'

"So, approaching my words made me retreat from you."

"We followed you in your conquests. But all we retain of your adventure is the vision of an inaccessible sky.

"We followed you in your search of yourself."

"I am responsible for the sky where my words, sometimes, evolve.

"You followed me when I had not chosen you. But without you, who am I."

"You are the narrator, Yukel. From book to book, from sky to sky."

"I am the stranger."

"Yukel, tell us the story of the stranger."

"I speak,
and you see through me,
you learn through my words,
and you follow the traitor who passes himself off as the servant, and without whom, alas (just as the giddy wind for the stem whose flower it tore off) Yukel, the stranger, would be nothing on earth but the nameless and unnecessary display of an instant of the unutterable distress."

2

I sailed in my stones so long that I became the
child of the five continents. And yet, I am only
the son of the old wall at whose foot I lament
with my brothers.

— Reb Angel

"The word of the voyage is subject to the wind."

— Reb Taleb

"Green, grey, black: the color of your words is that of the
road."

— Reb Mahler

("God disdains memory. He travels."

— Reb Haim

"The journey refuses the word.
One is silent in order to listen."

— Reb Accobas

"You travel to find the word of God. And until
then you stifle your words."

— Reb Benlassin)

"You came, and our tree blossomed."

— Reb Hillel

"I am no longer with myself.
I am with all of you.
With your foreheads. With your hands.
For the same tomorrows."

— Reb Avigdor

"Day is on your cheeks, night rings my eyes. I sleep against,
drowned in my light."

— Reb Rami

"Unreason is the Jew's vocation. It means believing in his
mission."

— Reb Doub

"The wind of freedom blows as hard as that of madness."
— Reb Houna

"In the hands of this man, there is a little soil of the country
he comes from."
"Ask him to bury it in our soil."
"In the hands of this man, there are some seeds for the soil
he comes from."
"Ask him to plant them in our soil."

"In the hands of this man, there is the silence of a child's
prayer."
"Ask him to build his house here."

— Reb Oda

"We can only be saved by ourselves. Such is our luck."
— Reb Mires

3

Do not ever forget that you are the kernel of a severance.

— Reb Armel

I

"Another day passes to give me a soul," said Reb Adon. "For death is at the threshold.

"Did not Reb Idal write: 'The heart is the soul of the dead?' "

"Do you mean to say we have no soul?" asked one of his disciples.

"We prepare ourselves for having one," replied Reb Adon, "like the pregnant woman for her child."

"In that case," continued the disciple, "when will we enjoy our soul?"

"When we will be one," said Reb Adon, "when we are born."

"Life is at its end," Reb Adon went on. "Life is at its end, I am sure of it . . . And at the end, there is nothing."

And Reb Aki: "When your blood coagulates, when your body turns cold, then the flowers swell and the trees spread their branches. And you, who were their fate, enter the sky where everything is white."

> (*"You want to take my name from me,"* said *Reb Eglia, one day, to his judges.* *"But with which other letters of our language would I face the nothing?"*
>
> *And Reb Lodé:* *"I live in a name with four walls. You can kill me. But what will you do with the stones of my dwelling fallen at your feet?"*)

"A blood stain, an ink stain, weigh more than a ton of corn."

"If ink has a reddish tinge, it is because it is mixed with blood."

"It is harder to turn the pages of the book of days than to move a building."

— Reb Elias

II

"God reveals Himself: an imagination prey to the loss of its image."

— Reb Sachs

"I know you, Lord, in the measure that I do not know you. For You are He who comes."

— Reb Lod

"My God, I am reduced to You.
I have exiled the word."

— Reb Pinhas

"Contradiction is the desire to oppose death to life in whatever is. One wants to be equal to the moment."

— Reb Sofer

III

"How shall I think about God, who is life, when I have so much to do with death, which is my future as a man."

— Reb Kob

"You deny God, because your love of Him has taken Him from your sight — just as light hides the light from us.

"Try to kill Him with your spears, and you will learn that He is the order of all resistance."

— Reb Sheba

"All roads are of flesh."

— Reb Achem

4

Death and life are perverted flowers. Their roots are in the mud of the sky and of being.

All rain is good for the soul, but bad for eternity, which has left life and death behind. Eternity, which is air.

One of the contemporary disciples of Reb Simoni reports the dialogue of twin flowers growing in his garden.

"I do not know," says the disciple of Reb Simoni, "if my garden is Heaven or Hell."

THE DIALOGUE OF THE TWO ROSES

"You have the nerve to challenge me in my soul."

"I am faithful to love."

"Love only loves itself."

"I am life. He is mine."

"Not always. Lovers give me their lives."

"Unhappy lovers. Not love."

"Love is the trap you set for men, so you can dress in their shivers and steep in their tears."

"Radiant eyes: that is what love is."

"Love devours those eyes which see."

"You are a cold friend."

"Yes, my accomplice." ("At this point, there was a long silence," notes Reb Simoni's disciple. "Then the voice became urgent:") "Let me have Sarah and Yukel."

"I do not want to lose them."

"Some day you will have to give in."

"Some morning maybe, when I feel gay, the moment I cannot stand them any more." ("Here, I thought I heard them giggling," notes Reb Simoni's disciple.) "There will be hours, maybe weeks, when you can tear them from me."

"You are cruel. You know they are suffering."

"Love is my youth."

"You are life."

"Love is the master of life."

"Let me have Sarah and Yukel."

"Why the hurry? Do you like them that much? You toady like a slave. Are you in love?"

"I have no use for love."

"Then why do you want my lovers?"

"Because it is part of the established order, and because it is my job."

"You make short work. And my pleasure? You do not care about that any more? I am disappointed."

"I sometimes feel affection for human beings."

"Why?"

"Out of pity, a little. Also, I like to be considered good."

"You are jealous. You are dying with love."

"I kill whatever I touch."

"Your body is drunk with the caresses, your petals moist with the kisses you expect. But I am strong. I am stubborn. I enjoy making you wait."

"You are set on hurting me. Be careful. I might take revenge."

("Here, it seemed to me," notes Reb Simoni's disciple, "they had come closer to one another. Their attitude was defiant.")

"Admit that I please you, that it is me you want through the couples who worship me."

("They turned their backs, only to face each other again, a few seconds later, with unfettered hatred," notes Reb Simoni's disciple.)

"Slut."

"What a nice admission."

"I am not at the end of my resources. You hurt me. You know it. I am torn by desire. Too bad. Too bad. Too bad. That is my business."

"I despise you."

"I love you with an impossible love. I will kill those who keep me from embracing you. I will make skylights of their eyes, lost ships of their bodies. The most sensual are the most vulnerable."

> ("A long moment must have passed which I have trouble remembering," notes Reb Simoni's disciple. "Bits of words came to my ear, but their sense escaped me. Then I distinctly heard:")

"Shut up. You make my blood run cold."

"You are snow which melts in April."

"I am fever. I am the sun. I hate water and shrouds."

"You die for each birth. You prepare creatures and world with great talent for their announced end. You are crazy to tell them about me. You are the antechamber. I am the bed. Your victims call to me for help. Their cries are pearls around my neck. I appear to them in my inaccessible splendor. I take possession of their eyes for good. I make a road of them, or a rainbow."

"Let me live. Let me feed on my life."

"Let me relish my death, prodigal rose."

> ("When I went over to make sure they were real," notes Reb Simoni's disciple, "I found myself in front of two roses open to a bee's greediness. They had resumed their plant life.")

"Yukel," wrote Sarah, "is it true that death seems preferable, today, to the best moments of our short lives?"

5

The burden of the Wandering Jew is an incorruptible voice.

— Reb Atem

I

"You come from Jerusalem, immense city, from which you have been chased a thousand times."

— Reb Jourda

"Out of a handful of sand we will make the beginning of a garden just as, since the exodus, we have made our sky out of all the grains of silence."

— Reb Ati

"Our flower, with its corolla of ashes, has as many petals as we have uttered screams."

— Reb Sholl

II

"In days of drought, the word is of water, and the face of a friend the cloud you hope for."

— Reb Mawas

"Salt everywhere. I am waiting for a little sweet water from the sky."

—Reb Kem

"Storm. My head is splitting. Friendship is killing me."
—Reb Zondek

"Water releases me from the word."

—Reb Hazac

III

"The love of my God is round. He created the earth with His love, so it would be round."

—Reb Dima

IV

"You will be the man I love so deeply that you will love me with my soul and my arms."

"I need you as life needs death in order to be reborn, and as death needs life in order to die."

—Sarah's Journal

"You know much. You love."

—Reb Racah

THE TIME OF THE LOVERS

Yukel: A blank page swarms with steps on the point of finding their own tracks. An existence is a scrutiny of signs.

Sarah: Is the dream not already death, Yukel? You bet on the margins, the clouds. Man carries time. We play against. Time is becoming, a second's blaze rekindled.

Yukel: Man is a merchant of ashes. Out of the world, I save the moment, my portion of eternity.

Sarah, my moment, my eternity.

Sarah: The word cancels out distance, drives space to despair. Is it really we who formulate it, or does it, rather, mold us?

Yukel: The hours tell man that he advances, whether lying down or standing, that he turns in circles like the hands of the clock—unaware that they are turning.

Daughters of the moon in their worry to light up a few inches of the universe, a fraction of the infinite, however minute, they have the coquetry of their sex and the jealousy of a jailer.

This morning, the hour was sublime light. The sun had mastered the dark. I had gotten up before dawn to witness a victory no doubt counted on, but unpredictable in its details. I watched the dismantling of the night, the capture of every single trench of shadow. What unsuspected cunning. What snares prepared in secret.

Words are windows, doors half open on to space. I divine their presence by their pressure against our palms, by the imprint they leave there.

Sarah: The sun conjugates life, in its visible diversion, through all the moods. Lovers prefer the night. They recognize each other by the shadow they bathe in like swimmers whose every muscle is caressed into hymns. At the bottom of the water, the heart is heard more clearly.

Yukel: Where are you, Sarah? My lady without manor, my river without banks. Your body does not hold you any more.

Sarah: I wrote you. I write you. I wrote you. I write you. I take refuge in my words, the words my pen weeps. As long as I am speaking, as long as I am writing, my pain is less keen. I join with each syllable to the point of being but a body of consonants, a soul of vowels. Is it magic? I write his name, and it becomes the man I love. All it takes to pass from night to day, and from day to night, is that a pen dipped in ink obey the movement of my hand, that the voice yield for a second to the whim of the lips, to the orders of thought. I hollow out a dwelling in desire. I write: "I am going to join you, my love . . ." And, instantly, I am wings which give me back my beloved. I say: "Be patient, my love . . ." and let the walls of my prison take me in again.

Yukel: I wrote you. I write you. I wrote you. I write you. I give you pet names, my little bird. I see you again in my hotel room, so upset by my departure. "Why? Why?" you pleaded. I see you again that last evening, some indifferent square between us. I see you running across the street between my hotel and your place. It is so dark.

Sarah: I wrote you. I write you. I wrote you. I write you. Write me, my love. I have lain in wait for the mailman all day long, as usual. Put my face on your avowals, chisel my shape in words. I am beautiful because I am the words which enhance me through your mouth. I am pale because your sadness lies on my cheeks. You write: "Your fingers are the paint brush of my hope." And my fingers grow, in their delight. You compare my arms to young waterfalls, my neck to a nest of timid birds, and I am water coming down the mountain, I am the cooing of the air imprisoned in its heart. My eyes open when you look at them. My breasts harden at your touch. Come, my beloved. Walk at my speed. We are our road.

Yukel: We move in ourselves, as the moon in the gold of its fine skin, as the current in the laugh of the river. Entangled, we are our universe. I had not thought our bodies were so vast, so deep. On the surface, they are two lovers: you and me. One can see them, talk to them. They do not take up much room. They cast a shadow in the morning. But enter into them, and they are giants the gods quarrel over. Beside itself, a being dwindles, draws in.

We are immense, Sarah. I am walking by your side.

Sarah: I write: "We are the signs gathered by our hands, the sounds uttered by our lips," and all of a sudden, a comma seems the image of a sigh, a full stop a border. We go from one sentence to the next, from one paragraph to the next, without realizing the number of miles covered.

Yukel: You are by my side, Sarah. I am swaying in the hammock woven by your perfume, slung from the dry branches of oblivion.

Sarah: I am the spring of oblivion. Lakes take our measure, like mirrors.

Where are you, Yukel? Words stick to my flesh as to blotting paper.

The world is illegible on the skin.

6

*The time of the earth is that of a question we
have tried in vain to answer.*

—Reb Diab

"God is a questioning of God."

—Reb Arwas

"Severed hand,
my five-fingered cup.
I drink what you hold
and am drunk."
—Reb Achim

"Our enemies have never all at the same time persecuted
us. So we have, now and then, found protection with a gener-
ous nation.

"But what a cruel game over the millennia, to save us a few
relays on our inevitable march around the earth."

—Reb Bosh

"A thousand times better to be downtrodden grass than a
flower transplanted," said Reb Risel. To which Reb Taba answered: "You are not dead, master. Is that not the main
thing?"

"Where do you come from, brother with the white face?"
"I come from that white part of the world where I was not."

"Where do you come from, brother with the dark skin?"
"I come from that black part of the world where I was not."

"Where do you come from, brother with the pale face and bent back?"
"I come from the boundless ghetto where I was born."

"Sit down for a moment, brother. Tomorrow, at sunrise, you will face a rough task."

—Reb Richon

A neighborhood lives through its streets, as the tree through the strength of its branches. A chessboard is the world of the city man. Have you noticed that every field, black or white, corresponds to an identical field in the sky? To go through a part of town means also going through a part of the night or the day. Here, you are at a certain crossing and at a certain imaginary intersection of the void.

You left Jerusalem in order to regain it. But your steps no longer annoy you. They vanish as soon as you have gone by. You need no longer turn around. Have you been walking that long?

The past has the voice of each imprint, each caress or wound we left around, in the ground, or in a creature. A room is filled with various noises, which silence puts in order. You listen to them the moment they approach the lamp to be burned like a swarm of voluptuous moths. Your body, as mine, responds with a thousand invisible marks whose history we are the only ones to know and not tell.

(The street awakens with the passer-by.
My street stirs in her sleep and speaks, now
softly, now loudly. My alley-way is an adolescent

*the middle of a noisy neighborhood, where her
sisters have lost the habit of rest.*

I watch her sleep.

*Each neighborhood has its star. And the star
seems tied to these walls like the cut flower to the
vase full of water.*

*The street has a name, which the passers-by
appropriate —*

*for the time it takes to leave her, to take an-
other name, in another street.*

*Absorbed in our thoughts, pressed by time or
destination, how often have we mistaken the
number of our steps for a street? For us, it is their
merit to be the shortest way to a certain place.
They canker in this limitation like small employ-
ees in an important firm. Some (is it revenge?) are
shrewish and narrow, always inclined to cover us
with labels.*

*There are many ways of becoming aware of a
street. If you just look at her from your window,
as one looks at a river flowing by, you lose her bit
by bit. Often, some banal incident, like suddenly
stopping in the middle of a sidewalk which can
hardly handle the flow of the crowd, being jos-
tled and pushed off, something like this may be
enough to reveal her to us in her misery or glory.*

*A street is never the same. She may be a quick
street, or slow, on certain days even lazy. In order
to be present in our houses, she resorts to traffic
noise or the puncturing silence of her sky and her
stones. — We do not pay attention to any of this
while we are part of it. But absent, she reigns
over our solitude, as oblivion (or its infinite
echoes) reigns over all things.)*

When the dark, by and by, gets a rosy tinge, I, Sarah, am already waiting for you to come. When the pink turns red and
yellow, I, Sarah, call you in vain. When the world is finally
white like the flame between our lashes, I, Sarah, look for you

in the nameless, chattering crowd. When dusk again falls over the world, I, Sarah, lose myself in you.

> *(What difference is there between love and loss? A fricative taken away, two sibilants added.*
> *I have lost it forever, my lovely v.*
> *I got in exchange the cruelest sound.)*

"It took all the intelligence of the heart to distinguish between Good and Evil."

— Reb Ivon

"To be two means being day, which is formed by morning and night."

— Reb Guened

The Book of the Living

First Part

In every stone, there is an appeal of the stone.

In every spring, there is an appeal of the water.

In every Jew, there is an appeal to the day.

For the stone can no longer stand to be stone.

The spring dreams forever of being held back.

The Jew expects each day to live.

1

*Wound me as you struck my forebears and my
father. I can only feed on my humiliated blood.*
— Reb Tobi

"The four seasons of man are hearing, sight, word, and
touch."

— Reb Atias

"One morning when we were lying on the beach, she traced
her initials in the sand with her forefinger.
S. S.
Sarah Schwall.
S. S.
S. S.

*(What was his name, Sarah? That young SS of-
ficer who wore your initials engraved in his soul,
who went everywhere thanks to your initials,
who wore a uniform designated by them?*

*What was his name, that young arrogant snob
without scruples, who derived his power from
the two capitals of your name?*

*He was not the only one to glory in the prestige
of this double letter.*

There were millions to glory with him.

How could you have resisted them inside your own name?

How could you have kept the other letters of your name from foundering, one after the other, in the sea of dead letters from which arose, brighter than dawn, the double letter called to rule the world, and which flouted the sun?

People did not see except through it. Whereas you and I and those like us in face and heart believed in the round sun, in the old time sun, which was theirs and the earth's.

 Sarah Schwall.
  arah chwall
  rah   wall
  S.   S.

Thus, a sheet of paper burns in the fireplace at home. Thus, a human being burns close to the mass grave. Thus, the memory of the loved one survives amid the ashes heaped up at your doors.

But the wind blows for your happiness, murderers.)

"You dread to see, and you see what you dread."

        — Reb Larish

"You speak, and suddenly you are a thousand words standing up."

        — Reb Leha

Sarah, there is no more day. Day is a long waiting. But will we see the end?

There is water under the bark of our years betrayed like abandoned fields.

How much courage is needed to think of the harvest? The dream of water is full of blades of wheat.

The drought is in the hearts.

"We can no longer correspond, Sarah. Tell me what you are thinking."

"I will tell you what you know — what you no longer know very well, perhaps. I am thinking of you with my new chains. I see you with eyes which have plunged into hell."

"You are at the age of sight. I am still at that of hearing."

"Listen, Yukel, listen. And I have only one wish: that you may never see what I see."

"You are at the age of the word, Sarah. And the word is taken from you. Through you, I slowly grow into the age of sight."

"Keep my hands in yours, Yukel. This is my only strength, my blessed chain."

"I open my arms, Sarah. I open my arms. Soon I shall enter my fourth season."

"Soon, Yukel, soon. For we have to cut our hands so that they can be born one from the other. Then they will be but the difficult road of the joined hands."

*I cannot accompany you home. I would have
to grant you the right to have a roof, which I
have always wanted.*

— Reb Mazlia

I

"Master," said Reb Vidor one day to Reb Goetz, "is it true
that the desert reaches down even into the soul? And that passion, which was originally a sand plant, pushes us to leave the
place of its past for a promise of woods or gardens?"

"The desert," replied Reb Goetz, "is the soul's awakening,
and sky, its envy. But the fruit of knowledge was plucked from
its own tree."

"Does the water bring up the tree like a mother her child?"

"For our unhoused voices, water is the reason for living."

"The word evolves between the sky and the earth, where
the future belongs to the branches. Should we not go to the
word, as the root rises to the fruit?"

"The garden means speaking, the desert, writing. In every grain of sand, a sign surprises us."

"Give us the lessons of your books to meditate on, master. So that for each page offered to the page, a word, learned at the heart of silence, may flower."

"My book is yours," answered Reb Goetz.

II

"I am the word within your reach,
"and timid.
"You call me.
"Would I know I will answer, if you stopped being sure?"

"You go in search of my love, and my love in search of you.
"How can we swear we will meet?"

"I believe in my love, which no longer recognizes me."

"I no longer know where I am. I know. I am nowhere. Here."

"I am like the candle panicked by the smallest breath.
"Do not move. Do not breathe.
"Tomorrow, the wax in the wick will fly."

"You are here. But this place is so vast that even being near means being so distant we can neither see nor hear each other."

—*Sarah's Journal*

The Book of the Living

Second Part

We walk barefoot along the pages of your book, Yukel, on rocks which overhang the sea. Your story is that of the waves, which break at our ankles and, sometimes, whip our faces. One and the same story, one and the same wave. Now full of strength, now so weak it seems wounded.

And we watch it, passively, because it asks nothing of us, but carries us beyond the shores, where the sun rises and sets, as if dark and light joined together for us.

Two words like two breasts

When the yellow star was shining in the sky of the accursed, he wore the sky on his chest. The sky of youth with its wasp's sting, and the sky with the armband of mourning.

He was seventeen. An age with wide margins.

And then one night, a little before day. And then one day, and then one night, and then nights, and days which were nights, the confrontation with death, the confrontation with the dawn and dusk of death, the confrontation with himself, with no one.

> *(From one night to the next, day is the hardest stage.*
> *At night, the curtains are drawn.*
> *He walks in the curtains.)*

When the yellow star was shining in the sky of the accursed, he wore the sky on his chest.

From one night to the next, day is the hardest stage.

When she was fourteen, Sarah wanted to be a teacher. Instead of joining her classmates on holidays, she gathered children around her, whom she taught to use words (to let themselves be caught by them), whom she told stories of light and dark. They listened, as one might listen to the colors of the world monologuing until evening.

Sarah took them up to her room. They liked best sitting on her bed. She stood before them, miming the tales of the opening of her roses, counting with them on her fingers, spelling the sources.

Childhood is a colony of words, which the years are set on dispersing.

When the yellow star was shining in the sky of the accursed, they wore the sky on their chests.

Childhood is a colony of astonished words.

> ("Sarah, Sarah, is this here the beginning of the world?"
>
> "We don't want to miss out on anything."
>
> "Is today the creation of the world? It is, isn't it?"
>
> "The world has been created."
>
> "But wasn't it destroyed?"
>
> "Sarah, Sarah, what was the first thing in the world?"
>
> "The word?"
>
> "Looking?"
>
> "Tell us, what was first?"
>
> "What, Sarah? Do tell."

"The world is a whole."

"Is it round like the head?"

"Round like a hoop? Just a circle?"

"But the woods, Sarah?"

"Yes, and school, Sarah?"

"Yes, yes, and the sea and the mountains?")

She does not know any more if he followed her. They had slowed down as if, together, they had become aware of a possible future.

"Your voice," he had said, "reminds me of my sister's."

"I had forgotten my voice," she had answered. Then, after an oppressive silence (it had seemed to her they were bending over it, as if to drink, after a long effort, the water of an invisible fountain): "My name is Sarah."

"There is no way out of this situation," Sarah had said. "A situation without grass, without leaves."

He had replied, "I love you."

"I love you," he had repeated.

Sunny mornings always have reasons to believe, which we are only too ready to share.

"Perhaps," Sarah had added softly.

There are people who think to found their future on certitudes, and others who know in advance they are building on sand.

"Listen. The wind is back," Sarah had said.

> *("I have had much experience with the wind,"* wrote Reb Medrar.
> *"There is the wind which blows outside, and the wind which blows within us.*

"With my own eyes, I have seen hearts and
brains which were nothing but a heap of rubble.
   "This spectacle is much more tragic than that
of devastated land.")

"Listen to the wind," said Sarah.

The image Sarah had of her grandparents Schwall was that
of an immobile, nearly grotesque couple whom she tried to
give voices to, without always succeeding. She had a photo-
graph of them, which the fingers of time had yellowed: absence always leaves its fingerprints.

Her father had all faces for her. He was a born storyteller.
How she would have loved to be like him. She admired him
through his stories, so familiar in their strangeness that she
could have lived them.

"Moses," said Sarah's mother to her husband, when she had
enough or wanted to send her daughter to bed, "will you
never stop identifying with Yukel Serafi?"

But Sarah insisted: "Go on, father." She was greedy for lies
and made them her daily bread: "Tell me about Yukel Serafi,
father. I love his stories."

And her father said: "Be patient. One day, you will invent
them."

Salomon Schwall had come from Corfu. He left his island at
an early age, married, in Portugal, the younger daughter of a
rabbi and settled with her, at thirty-one, in the South of
France, as an antique dealer.

When he went walking, with his hands behind his back, his
eyes (especially outside the town) kept searching the ground,
prodding into it. No obstacle rebuffed him. His eyes spread
the arms and legs of the ground in order to bury his seed.
Need for roots. Need to recognize himself, to be recognized, a
creature, a plant, a presence of this soil in its whole sweep, a
living element of the landscape. Need to be reborn of it.

His shop, "The Thousand Things," an honest (as it called

attention to it) ambush for the people passing through the Avenue du Centre, held at first few objects for sale. But the repainted walls came relatively fast up to the promise of the name. Indeed, a thousand things, from silver candle sticks to embroidered screens, from eighteenth century chests ("of course, it is genuine") to settees and a bewildering bric-a-brac of angels, bronze and plaster statues, chandeliers, ivory miniatures, tables, armchairs, ancient mirrors and medals, fabrics and tapestries, were offered to the curious and overwhelmed customers.

Salomon Schwall died, with his eyes raised to the light. At the end of his life, resigned to his fate as foreigner, he had discovered the sky and felt no more attraction to the ground which rejected him. Salomon Schwall died questioning the firmament. His wife, a worried and washed-out woman, survived him only by a few days. She had a materialistic idea of fidelity, summed up by the saying: "The way to a man's heart is through his stomach," which, in fact, she liked to quote. It was a way of bragging without seeming to, because she was famous for her cooking and, apparently, Salomon had not disappointed her in his affection.

She passed away, her eyes in the sheets.

Their only son, Moses, was taken in by a maternal uncle in the capital, served in the infantry, then, after the war, traveled around the world on the steamers of the *Messageries maritimes,* first as a deck boy, then as a cabin boy, lived for some years in Africa, met Rebecca Sion in Cairo, fell in love, and married her.

From his father, Moses Schwall inherited eyes consoled by the horizon, from his mother, eyes that keep company with the ground.

From her deported parents as well as from her companions in captivity, Sarah inherited the stubbornness of her race.

"I am burning," she said, one day, to a companion. "I am burning, Abel, and you do not see me. You see the night."

"I belong to another world," he replied, "which I have all these years been learning to face. You cannot understand. You are alive. On you, fields of wheat are stretching which will produce a better bread.

"But God will die in the conflagration."

"Eat my bread, Abel," she shouted at him. "Eat my bread, which I baked in the fire which killed your God."

When the yellow star was shining in the sky of the accursed, they were the sky where the yellow stars burned out, the sky of the past and the sky of the future.

They were the line of chance
and zigzagging failure.

> ("*Revolt is a crumpled page in the waste bas-ket,*" *wrote Reb Tislit.* "*But, often, a masterpiece is born from this sacrificed page.*"
>
> *And Reb Ezé:* "*True revolt is the one inspired by the impossibility of ending. God is in perpet-ual revolt against God.*"
>
> "*In this case, I renounce the God who has sac-rificed the smile,*" *said Yukel.*)

Silence envelops the city, with its buildings leaning on one another: gigantic boxes, from some of which light gleams through a haphazard opening, maybe from a blow.

He thinks of the various processions he has taken part in, pa-rades, forced marches.

We fall into line and follow.

We do not see the face of those in front, but we know it was once ours.

It is behind this face that we age, that we let time escape, that we take leave.

"I, for my part, belong to a generation without face," said Yukel.

They were the line and the failure.

I speak in time and out of time.
I speak for yesterday and today.
For yesterday, which is a lesson of life.
For today, which is a lesson of death.

I could have been this man. I have put on his uniform.
"We both have the number of our expiration tattooed on our forearms."

At that time, barbed wire grew like ivy, but round, round and deep.

This circle is worth stopping at, worth a close look.

You think you are alone in yourself, caught between meshing saw-teeth. But soon you notice there is a whole tribe identifying with the wheel, conforming to the routine spirit of the wheel.

"Yukel, tell us of this absurd, infernal round."
"I will tell you of the evidence in tow of the daggers."

There are as many evidences as there are retinas. But the eyelids know when to use their power as shutters.

At that time, evidence was queen. You could admire her, applaud. She got daily fatter. She had her body guard and her army. Her courtiers and ministers.

At that time, the ashes of Jews sent to the ovens were used to season her meals.

"Close your eyes," advised the sensitive souls.

"Do not look away," pleaded the victims.

The door which opened onto the mass grave or onto life was the triangle formed by our conquerors' legs. You had to get down on all fours to go through it. Honor to those who were trampled there. Honor to those whose skulls were cracked by the boots of the enemy parading in rhythm to his hymns of glory. They interrupted the rhythm of his song, if only for a moment. They hindered the unfolding of the sound. Victory is in fullness. One false note, one note missing, and the edifice crumbles.

Evidence had killed surprise.

Everything became evident.

> *(Evident the morning.*
> *Evident the dark.*
> *Evident the fault.*
> *Evident the duty.)*

And Serge Segal shouted at the prisoners around him, who would soon be scattered in the various extermination camps prepared for them, shouted as if in the name of the Lord to His assembled people: "You are all Jews, even the anti-Semites, because you are all marked for martyrdom. Your future is mine, docile pain for those who are prepared. I pity and kiss you, brothers. Your eyes recite in chorus the prayer of the mornings of misfortune."

3

The light of Israel is a scream to the infinite.

The fence can be seen from afar. The house, with its roof (which the clouds fear because it looks deceptively like a cloud), with its closed doors and windows, dominates the madwoman's path, which noone else walks.

"That madwoman," asked Sarah, "is she really dead?"

"The scream you heard was an owl. Let's go back in. It's late."

The women in the village made the sign of the cross. The men fell silent long enough to identify the scream and shrug.

"There she goes again."

"There she goes again."

The fence can be seen from afar. It is in flower. The seasons are born and die in the ground.

"There she goes again," said Léonie Lull, turning her head towards the hill. "There she goes again.

"Even in my sleep I hear her."

"Even when she does not scream, I hear her," said Mathilde Meyvis.

The madwoman's house sleeps in its cradle rocked by

the nurse's hands. The madwoman's house rocks amid trees hidden by their leaves.

We have to cut off the hands,
have to fell the trees
to destroy the madwoman's house in its cradle.

We must wake her.

The water you float on, the water you give in to, is the water of sleep.

The water you wash in, the water you fight against, is the water of awakening.

Madness keeps awake
the madwoman's sleep,
but never wakes her.

The madwoman sleeps and moves, makes gestures and sleeps (makes her sleep make gestures), speaks and sleeps (makes her sleep speak).

"There she goes again."
"There she goes again."

"That madwoman," asked Sarah, "is she really dead?"

"As the dark is pierced by the light, the soul is pierced by the scream," wrote Reb Seriel.

And Reb Louel: "The Jewish soul is the fragile casket of a scream."

Madness keeps awake
the madwoman's sleep,
but never wakes her.

"That owl," asked Sarah, "is it really me?"
"The scream you heard was an owl. Let's go back in. It's late."

"I do not hear the scream," said Sarah. "I am the scream."

(The lives of one or two generations of men may fill one sentence or two pages. The gross outline of four particular or ordinary lives: "He was born in . . . He died in . . . " Yes, but between the scream of life and the scream of death? "He was born in . . . He was insulted for no good reason . . . He was misunderstood . . . He died in . . . " Yes, but there must be more? "He was born in . . . He tried to find himself in books . . . He married . . . He had a son . . . He died in . . . " Yes, yes, but there must be more? "He was born on . . . He gave up books . . . He thought he would live on in his son . . . He died on . . . " Yes, but there must be more? "He was short and heavy-set . . . He had a childhood and an old age . . . His name was Salomon Schwall . . . " Yes, yes, but there must be more? "His name was Salomon Schwall . . . He does not remember his youth . . . He left his island . . . He went to Portugal . . . His wife was called Léonie . . . " Yes, yes, but there must be more? "He settled in the South of France with his wife . . . He was an antique dealer . . . He was called 'the Jew' . . . His wife and son were called 'the wife and the son of the Jew.' " Yes, but there must be more? "He died, and his wife died . . . They were buried in ground which did not know their names, near some crosses . . . " Yes, but there must be more? "His son was French . . . He fought in the war for France . . . He was decorated . . . " Yes, yes, but there must be more? "He fought in the infantry . . . was wounded . . . decorated . . . " Yes, yes, but there must be more? "He was still called 'the Jew' . . . He married Rebecca Sion, whom he met in Cairo . . . He went back to France with her . . . " Yes, but there must be more? "He became a merchant in memory of his

father . . . He had brought back all sorts of ob-
jects from his travels . . . Oceanic and African
masks . . . pottery and gemstones from China,
carved ivory from Japan . . . " Yes, but there must
be more? "He had a daughter, Sarah . . . " Yes,
but there must be more? "He was still called 'the
Jew,' and his wife and daughter, 'the wife and
the daughter of the Jew.' " Yes, yes, but there
must be more? "He had lost his faith . . . He no
longer knew who he was . . . He was French . . .
decorated . . . His wife and daughter were French
. . . " Yes, but there must be more? "Sometimes,
he spoke in public to brand racism, to affirm the
rights of man . . . " Yes, yes, but there must be
more? "He died in a gas chamber outside France
. . . and his wife died in a gas chamber outside
France . . . and his daughter came back to France,
out of her mind . . . ")

The madwoman's house sleeps in its cradle, rocked by the
nurse's hands. The madwoman's house rocks amid trees hidden by their leaves.
   We have to cut off the hands,
   have to fell the trees
to destroy the madwoman's house in its cradle.
   We must wake her.

"One is the only one to know one's life," said Moses
Schwall. "And one's life is a breath."

"The owl howling against the wind," asks Sarah, "is it me,
Yukel, is it me? The owl against the wind, the owl for the
wind? Is it me, Yukel, is it me? The wind sweeping off my
screams, my screams exasperating the wind?"

4

Does seeing mean forgetting what one has seen?

Now is the time to defend our word.

> ("*Listen to the words in your heart, which your tongue is ready to take over,*" *said Reb Zilon.* "*But you must hinder it, for fear of losing your life. We are condemned to speak only for ourselves.*"
>
> *And Reb Lates:* "*I discovered the tongue and the lips of my heart. Since then, I have not had a mouth.*
>
> "*You consider me taciturn, while I am really a hive of words.*")

Now is the time to defend our mouths, the day to proclaim our red freedom.

> ("*How much blood!*" *said Reb Aslan.* "*And its insane idea in our speeches.*"
>
> *And Esther Eskeil:* "*My wedding dress was ripped off by our hangmen. Do you not see that I am crawling naked over bloody ground?*")

Now is the time to defend our bed.

> *("He died on his name," said Reb Dob, "on let-*
> *ters so transparent that he seemed to lie on the*
> *tracks left by a cloud.*
> *"But his bed is infinite.")*

"Master," said Reb Zaccai to Reb Denté, "you are a strange navigator. You explore the visible and invisible worlds claimed by the universe. And the ocean is ink for your pen."

"Words," answered Reb Denté, "have inherited the seven seas which quarrel over the continents, and the seven seas which conjugate the seven times of the blue fervor of the sky.

"Writing means going on a journey, at the end of which you will not be the same,

at the bottom of the page filled."

When he thinks of his parents, they appear from the other bank. Between them, the red river which has carried so much mud; between them, all the mud the blood has carried.

He rarely thinks of them. His childhood was chopped off prematurely, his adolescence stabbed in the neck, like the bull in the arena. His adolescence is a neck wounded ten times, then finished off with the sword.

He was cheated out of his parents' death. They were born for him — they died without him, perhaps for him. They died among their fellows, and their last glance was, no doubt, also for them.

They did not have time to appreciate him, to judge him (but do parents judge their children?) to like or deplore the person he became. Their relation began with "Yukel, come here. Don't do that, Yukel." (His earliest memories.) And it ended, one morning, with "We have to separate, Yukel. It's better to be prudent." (His last memory.)

All memories are bound to death.

He thinks of his sister dead in his arms, of the locked as-phyxiated land, of all the dead who delight in Sarah's mad-ness, of Sarah, dead in the life of grain and fruit.

5

Yesterday, like a full stop.

*("In the morning, you count your pennies, and
you do not know what the morning has in store
for you. You count three pennies:
one penny for your hunger,
one penny for your thirst,
one penny for nothing."*

— Reb Jol

*"The Nothing is our main care," said Reb Idar.
"We often sacrifice to it the finest hours we
hoped for.")*

This morning, words loot the flowers, and sentences crawl
in the mud like worms. Nothing takes shape or form outside
the word.

The butterfly is entrusted with the name of the flower, the
worm with that of the stem or trunk.

I am butterfly and worm.

This morning, nothing takes shape or form outside me.

I am furrow and word. I am my land, expressed.

*("More than a land, we need a language in
common, our language, that of our ancestors, for*

our sons to propagate. It will return to them the
loaded dice of their destiny."

—Reb Shames)

"Once we have a fatherland, we will love it with all the
strength of our lost loves. Our words will be hymns."

—Reb Panigel

"Let us lift up our voices, brothers. Let them be our dome."

—Reb Hila

I did not look for you, Sarah. I did look for you. Through
you, I go back to the sources of the sign, to the unformulated
writing the wind sketches on the sand and on the sea, to the
wild writing of the bird and the mischievous fish. God, the
Master of the wind, Master of the sand, Master of the birds and
fishes, expected from man the book, which man expected from
man. The one, in order to be finally God, the other, in order to
be finally man. The book of the order of the elements, the
unity of the universe, of God and of man.

Through you, Sarah, I have gone back to the language of the
night, to the very first attempts of the blind word frantic to see,
impatient to take form around its sensual significance, frantic
to fly with its own wings. The word, hairy like the bee's body,
which the day lies in wait for, and which anticipates the day.

Through you, Sarah, I go back to the bee and the day, which
is not, but which is coming soon, to the rose, which is not, but
which has been announced to the earth.

Tomorrow, Sarah, the dawn will have stolen your mouth,
stolen your breasts, stolen your thighs.

Tomorrow, our tears will be our pearls, and your hair our
time.

I did not look for you. I did look for you. Within me, sunny

landscapes requested that you come. Fertile fields pleaded for
my arm, expected to be nourished by me in order to nourish
me in turn.

The open air, the joys of a simple and healthy world were
within my reach. A world where words are fruit, syllables
branches and stems, where silence fuses with the roots. Why
not? A world where I only had to show myself in order to be
tanned golden by the sky, as if there were no more walls or
barbed wire, but only the space of happiness to take and give
back to the people who allowed it. I told myself it was my due,
because I needed it. I also told myself that this must be the
same happiness, the same joy, my brothers from central Eu-
rope had felt when, after having fled their ghetto (their fatherland which fitted all inside the ghetto), they found themselves, one morning, in the heart of the East, responsible for a
piece of land which two thousand years of oblivion had struck
off the earth. Did they have the right to be there? One right
certainly: the right to the open air, to the space they had been
deprived of. But at what price?

Within me, not everything was ruins or traces of ruins. My
childhood kept hold of its gleam of marbles, its innocence of
hopscotch and playing Indian, beyond death.

I did not look for you, Sarah. I did look for you in the laby-
rinth of my night, in the heart of total night, where mere ap-
prehension of wounds had by and by turned into wounds, an
enclosure of wounds not to be bandaged, but endlessly re-
opened.

I did not look for you. I had looked for you for a long time. I
had remembered to my cost that, to have a shepherd, there
must be a herd and, to satisfy a wolf's hunger, there must be
sheep. We were perfect sheep whose wool is taken: heads and
bodies shaven, even our souls.

You could save me, Sarah.

Behind us, there was laughter still in a state of buds;
before us, goodbyes which showed us the way. And suddenly, I saw you and felt that, helping you, I helped myself. Because you were too fragile to carry alone the

weight of your yellow star. And I was too alone to stray from the herd.

You could save me, Sarah, resuscitate my childhood, give arms to my adolescence, make me a man.

I did not look for you, Sarah. I did look for you. And suddenly you appeared to me in the wake of your eyes open to the world, your eyes, start of the round spectrum of the future, pulling the past out of the dark to hold it in the less solitary region of half-light, where it could be made out and approached.

I did not look for you, Sarah. I did look for you. You were going to save me. We had lost, you understand? I was going to save you. In you, everything testified that not all was lost.

And I read in you, through your dress and your skin, through your flesh and your blood. I read, Sarah, that you were mine through every word of our language, through all the wounds of our race. I read, as one reads the Bible, our history and the story which could only be yours and mine.

Also, when I spoke to you, I knew you could not refuse to answer. Because, as my phrases burned my lips, the anticipated, ready answers to them burned yours.

We were going to talk, Sarah, finally talk, after months and years of useless words or silence. We were going to talk in order to hear one another, understand one another, in order to unite.

And with our words, we were going to repeople the world, people it with friends, beings, brotherly objects and responses: "Yes. Yes. Yes." Unanimous acceptance of our anxious invitations. "Yes" to our hunger and to that of the world. "Yes" to our timid smile and the cautious smile of the world. "Yes. Yes. Yes," wherever people had said "No" to people, wherever worlds had said "No" to our world.

We were going to shape and live, in the name of life, with our minds and hearts, the truth we had invented.

*(Truth is incessant invention since it con-
tradicts itself, since only the provisional is
true, only what can be shared. As soon as our
eyes rest on a thing, on a landscape, as soon
as the emotion induced by these half-seen
things has us in its grip, they change. We
gave them the life they solicited. Their past
fuses with our first surprise. They only exist
through us, for us. Outside us, they exist for
all that is not them and metamorphoses them.
Thus, God ceases to be eternal by living
within us. But it is to the billions of succes-
sive lives of God within the lives of men that
He owes his eternity and life.)*

We were going to live our immense truth.

Have you seen how a word is born and dies?
Have you seen how two names are born and die?
From now on, I am alone.
The word is a kingdom.
Every letter has its quality, its grounds, and its rank.
The first holds the greatest power, power of fascination
and obsession. Omnipotence is its lot.
Sarah.
Yukel.
United kingdoms, innocent worlds, which the alphabet con-
quered and then destroyed through the hands of men.
You have lost your kingdom.
I have lost my kingdom, as my brothers have, scattered ev-
erywhere in a world which has feasted on their dispersion.
Have you seen how a kingdom is made and unmade?
Have you seen how a book is made and unmade?